handywoman's
workbook

handywoman's
workbook

how to do it yourself without breaking a nail

Bridget Bodoano

BARNES
&NOBLE
BOOKS
NEW YORK

This edition published by Barnes & Noble, Inc.
by arrangement with Quadrille

2004 Barnes & Noble Books

M 10 9 8 7 6 5 4 3 2 1

ISBN 0-7607-5352-0

Editorial Director Jane O'Shea
Creative Director Mary Evans
Art Director Helen Lewis
Designers Katy Davis and Jim Smith
Project Editor Lisa Pendreigh
Text Editor Nicki Marshall
Special Photographer Graham Atkins Hughes
Picture Researcher Nadine Bazar
Illustrators Bridget Bodoano and Coralie Bickford-Smith
Production Controller Beverley Richardson

Printed and bound in Singapore

contents

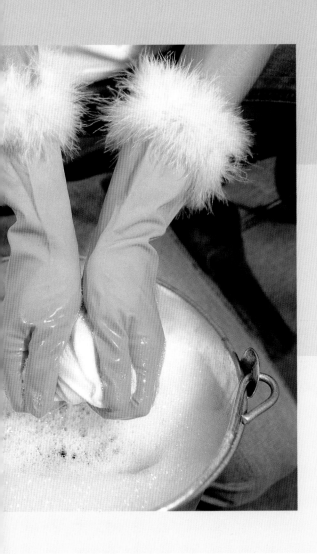

introduction

The traditional division of labor with men putting up shelves while grateful women clean up the mess now seems quaint as well as decidedly politically incorrect. There is plenty of evidence that today's women are putting up their own shelves—and that men are discovering the joys of housework.

The enormous increase in the number of single households means that a large proportion of women have no "man about the house" and so must remain shelf-less unless they are prepared to Do It Themselves.

Of course, many women have perfectly nice men around the house, but not all of them are skilled handymen—after all, insisting that all men are naturally handy with a hammer is as politically incorrect as suggesting that women should stick to dusting. Others, tired of standing by their man, dutifully passing the tape measure, drill, anchor plugs, screws, and screwdriver have taken the comparatively small step to using the tools themselves.

However, while the numbers of women getting involved in home improvement is rising steadily there are still a lot of modern, emancipated ones who, though they can simultaneously program a cell phone and download a complicated system onto a computer, have yet to come to grips with a hammer or a power drill.

Equally, the old-fashioned, pipe-smoking, home handyman dad, who once would have taken pride in teaching his offspring the best way to hold a chisel, has been replaced by modern, denim-clad dad, much too busy tinkering with his sound system or his motorcycle to be bothered with brackets and bradawls.

The old image of home improvement as a "hobby," with enthusiasts spending every weekend ruining perfectly nice homes with inappropriate, unwise, unattractive, and unsuccessful repairs and remodeling, has been replaced with a new sexier image, which is all about making the best of your home and creating a personal space to suit your needs as well as your personality and particular passions.

The new look for modern interiors is essentially simpler and pared down, with the

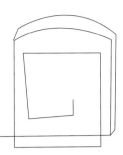

emphasis on the space and the structural qualities of a room or building. Achieving this often involves taking out the previous occupants' outdated, tacky attempts at home "improvements" in order to restore calm and dignity to abused properties.

The advice and information in this book is intended to encourage you to use basic tools and skills to repair and prepare your home for inspired decoration and stylish additions. The decorating techniques are intended to encourage and inspire you to take on simple projects and perhaps consider more major improvements to your home.

Doing it yourself is very satisfying, plus you benefit from knowing that the job has been done well—often at a fraction of the cost of employing a professional. However, not all jobs around the home can be done by beginners and some should only be carried out by a qualified expert. By learning something of the wonders and mysteries hidden behind walls and under floors, and the sorts of problems that can arise when carrying out repairs and improvements, you will be able to judge whether to do it yourself or whether to leave it to the experts.

handywoman essentials

the guide to tools and materials

Shopping for tools can be as pleasurable as shopping for clothes, with the added bonus that, in comparison, everything seems such a bargain. For the price of a designer label T-shirt you can buy a whole set of tools that will last for years, won't shrink in the wash, and won't go out of fashion. Power tools are a lot cheaper than power dressing and you can varnish a whole floor for the price of a month's worth of manicures.

The ambience of a large home improvement store may not be quite as stylish as a local boutique, but it has a buzzy, busy atmosphere. First visits can be a bit daunting, but many stores have a policy of providing plenty of staff willing to guide you through a job and advise on the tools and equipment needed to carry it out. In fact, in the world of home improvement there is no shortage of advice. Make friends with the staff in your local hardware store. Faced with serving grumpy contractors and other professionals for most of the day, they will be only too happy to explain how, why and what to buy—and may throw in a few good jokes and the odd discount as well.

Many of the large home improvement stores cater mainly for the amateur. They have all the products that make the jobs easier with tools and materials that make it possible for nonprofessionals to take on ambitious projects. Many stores also produce excellent how-to brochures that give detailed instructions along with clear drawings and useful tips. However, some of the easy-to-do solutions lead to less than stylish results, so be discriminating in your choice of materials. Keep to simple jobs using good-quality, good-looking components.

Choosing which tools and materials to buy is made very difficult by the widely differing prices for what, at first glance, seem to be very similar products. For items such as basic hand tools the quality will be reflected in the price: for a beginner the cheaper ones are usually perfectly adequate. For anything that involves machinery, motors, or electricity, it is better to go for a well-known, reputable brand as they will conform to the required standards and safety regulations. Own-brand decorating materials are often inexpensive; many of them are extremely good value and not that different than the well-known brands. However, some inexpensive paints are often thinner and therefore need extra coats, while products such as crack-filling compounds are just not as good as the more expensive versions. Trial and error is one way to find out but don't be afraid to ask staff or even other shoppers. There is a camaraderie among home improvement enthusiasts that can lead to friendly conversations in the plumbing aisle or even long-term relationships!

10 basic hand tools

There are a huge number of fancy and frightening-looking tools on the market, but most basic home improvement jobs can be done with a select few. The difficult part is deciding which of the hundred or so screwdrivers hanging on the store racks is the one for you. Good quality is important, but expensive tools are usually for professionals or picky purists. There are many perfectly good tools at very reasonable prices.

bradawl
A short, sharp spike sticking out of a chunky handle. Used for marking the position and making a small pilot hole for nails, screws, and hooks.

claw hammer
No toolbox is complete without one. Used for knocking in nails, but more frequently for taking them out. Invaluable for minor demolition work.

screwdrivers
There are two main types: the slotted, which has a flat tip and is used for screws with a straight slot in the head, and the cross-head or Philips, which is used for screws with a cross-shaped slot. You will need both types, which come in various sizes and lengths. For faster screwing there are power screwdrivers. They save energy and screw tighter, and in reverse gear their other great function is taking out screws.

utility knife
The classic utility knife has a chunky, easy-to-grip handle with strong replaceable blades that come in a variety of shapes. Used for cutting everything from cardboard to carpet.

tape measure
A metal retractable tape measure can be used for measuring rooms or marking smaller distances. A medium-width 10-foot-long tape measure will fit nicely in your hand.

wrenches
For tightening, and undoing, nuts and bolts. Adjustable wrenches can be altered to fit any size bolt but are a bit unwieldy. A set of wrenches isn't too expensive.

saws
Buy an all-purpose handsaw for cutting wood and plastics. Also invest in a small hacksaw with a thin, replaceable blade which is useful for cutting metal and plastic pipes.

carpenter's level
An intriguing device that shows whether surfaces and edges are truly horizontal and vertical. Essential for putting up shelves.

try square
Consists of a ruled metal straight-edge set at exactly 90 degrees to a straight piece at one end. Useful for marking lengths of wood and checking right angles.

pliers
For gripping objects so that you can turn, squeeze, pinch, or pull out a variety of things from nails in awkward corners to screw tops that won't unscrew. Blunt-nose pliers are good for general use but the long-nose variety are useful for intricate jobs.

10 tool tips

Treat yourself to a snazzy box or bag with compartments or pockets to store your tools.

Make sure your tools are easily accessible.

Always put tools back in their box or bag once you have finished with them.

Keep manufacturer's instructions with the tools.

Buy a power drill that comes in a handy box with space for its bits.

Keep all sharp blades covered when not in use.

Carefully throw away all old disposable blades.

Always keep a pair of gloves, safety glasses, a dust mask, and some bandaids in your toolbox.

Keep a set of screwdrivers and wrenches together in their original packaging or in a pocketed roll.

For a safe and comfortable grip, always choose power tools that fit your handsize and are not too heavy.

girl power

Power tools are a great boon to handywomen. Although these weaponlike objects may look a bit frightening, they are surprisingly easy to use providing you choose ones that are suited to your capabilities and stature. What can be difficult is choosing which ones to buy. The variety of power tools on offer range from screwdrivers to large circular saws, with a few snazzy multifunction options in between. They come in many shapes, sizes, and colors but don't be guided by looks—some of the best-looking are low-powered or only designed for specialist tasks.

The range of tools on sale in most home improvement stores is large while information is scarce, so do a little research first. Browsing through the internet is a good way to discover the function, power, and speed of products. Many companies offer a helpline where assistants dispense good advice (and don't mind in the least if you're not an expert).

getting tooled up

There are several tempting-looking power tools on the market, but initially try to resist buying anything other than a power drill. Planers, circular saws, and belt sanders need a higher level of skill and can always be rented if necessary. A jigsaw, however, is not too difficult to use and will give a neater, straighter cut than a handsaw, with a lot less effort.

To start with, invest in a power drill: you won't be able to make holes in solid walls without one. Today, even the most basic power drill possesses many capabilities that were once only available on professional models including high power, variable speed, hammer action, and reverse gear. Some can be used as screwdrivers and a range of accessories can be added for sanding and polishing.

Motor power is expressed in volts: the higher the voltage the more powerful and versatile the drill. They usually range from 6 volts to 14 volts; you will need around 14 volts if you want to drill into masonry. Low-powered drills don't usually have hammer action (see below).

Hammer action allows for easy drilling into hard surfaces. A simple rotary action is sufficient for making holes in wood, but for masonry a hammer or percussion action (which adds vibration as well as rotation) is necessary. Most new drills feature both, and selection is made with a switch or button.

The ability to vary the speed allows for more efficient drilling: most modern drills now have this facility. Speed is given in revs per minute and most general-purpose drills will go up to 3000 rpm. Slower speeds are needed for drilling into particularly hard surfaces, and faster speeds are used for wood to give a neat finish and prevent splitting. Most modern drills have variable speed control allowing you to set a speed suited to the material being drilled. A slow speed is also necessary if you want to use the drill as a screwdriver. Reverse is essential if you are going to use the drill to remove as well as drive screws. It also comes in handy if the drill bit gets stuck.

powering ahead

Power tools are driven by either electricity or by battery (cordless). Cordless drills were developed for use in places where there is no easy access to an electrical outlet, such as outside or up a tall ladder. While cordless drilling is undoubtedly convenient, there are disadvantages. With a battery the power is not consistent—it will lessen as the battery runs down—and it can be a hassle remembering to re-charge it. Buy a spare battery and keep it charged so it's ready for use when the first battery goes flat. Something that plugs in is usually just as convenient but be aware of the cord: don't get entangled in it and, if it is too short to allow free movement, use an extension cord.

boring facts

When drilling, the part that actually makes the hole is called a bit. Bought separately, the bit fits into the drill clamping device or chuck (a ring of claws that grip the bit firmly) which is then tightened.

If the drill has a keyed chuck the tightening is done with a chuck key. The key fits into three holes on the chuck and is turned until it won't go any farther (you need to tighten it in all three holes). A keyless chuck is tightened by turning the chuck itself after the spindle lock has been unlocked; this is usually done by pressing it in.

Bits come in a variety of shapes and sizes suited to different functions and materials. For simple jobs, you will use mainly twist bits (the straight ones with a thread) for drilling holes, but you need the right bit for the material used. A masonry bit is very tough and has a tungsten carbide tip. Wood bits have a sharp cutting thread and point for accurate positioning. Metal bits are made from hard steel and have a V-shaped tip but can also be used for wood.

The size of bit used will depend on the size of hole needed to accommodate the screw. Like screws, drill bits are sized by number: the smaller the number, the finer the bit. Both twist and masonry bits come in many sizes, with the most widely used ranging from $\frac{1}{8}$ inch to $\frac{3}{8}$ inch.

A countersink bit has a short, wide pointed end. It drills shallow cone-shaped recesses in wood for countersinking screws—that is, allowing the screw head to be flush with, or below the surface. Screwdriver bits include flat-tip and cross-head versions.

You can buy a set of drill bits that includes masonry, wood, and metal bits, as well as countersink and screwdriver attachments. They are inexpensive and usually come in a neat box for safekeeping. Other attachments for power drivers can turn them into a rotary sander, a polisher, or a rust remover.

in a fix

Looking for a simple nail or screw in a home improvement superstore can be a nightmarish experience as you wander up and down long aisles filled with a huge, confusing variety of sizes and shapes. Often there are helpful information panels above the merchandise explaining the different types and what they are used for. However, matching the diagrams to the actual products is not always straightforward, so if in doubt ask a salesclerk (or try asking the guy in dusty clothing and big boots standing next to you—he's probably a professional and may be delighted to recommend the right fixing for the job). Nails are easy to use and only require a suitable hammer and a steady hand to knock them into place, but most jobs are better done using screws which provide stronger grip and more support. Screws are also easy to unscrew if you make a mistake, want to take something down or move it to a different position. When you have found the basics you can then investigate the numerous ingenious fixings from cup hooks to coat hooks, heavy-duty gate hinges to tiny delicate box hinges, and a variety of feet, castors, rings, and knobs which will inspire and tempt you into taking on more adventurous tasks.

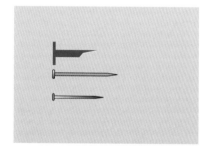

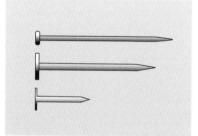

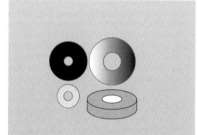

tacks
Short, tapered nails with a large head and sharp point. Easy to use. Mostly for securing carpet and fabric where the large head keeps it in place.

brads
Thin nails that have a small head or no head. Used when screws are too big and may split the wood, such as attaching panels. Go in easily and are barely visible.

nails
Available in a huge variety of shapes and sizes. Unless you are into real building work you will use mostly wire nails which are oval in cross section and have a solid, slim head. A lost-head nail has a head that is not much wider than the nail, is therefore less visible and can be knocked below the surface of the wood with a nail set.

washers
Disks of rubber, metal, or plastic with a hole in the middle. They have a variety of uses including forming a seal in plumbing, preventing a screw head or other fixing from penetrating too far into a material or protecting a surface or component from damage.

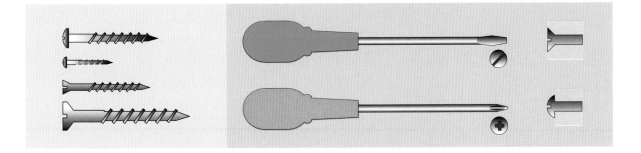

screws

More efficient than nails. Screws have a thread which bites into whatever material is being screwed into, giving a firm fixing. They come in various types and sizes which are described by length and diameter. The size you use depends on the use—thicker and longer for heavy jobs to bear a lot of weight and slimmer ones for thinner materials and lighter jobs. Brass screws are often used for good-quality wood as they look great. However, brass is weak and overtightening can shear off the screw head.

Screws are fixed by a screwdriver that fits into a slot in the screw head. There are two types—the "slotted head" with a straight groove across the center, and the "cross-head" or Philips with a cross-shaped indentation. A flat-tip screwdriver is used for slotted heads. A cross-head screwdriver has a pointed end that fits into the cross-shaped slot. There are various shapes of screw head but the most common are countersunk which will lie flush with the surface, and round-head which won't.

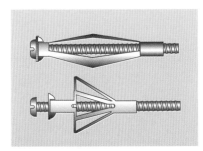

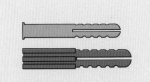

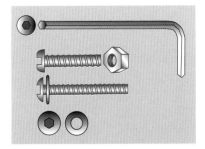

hollow wall and door fixings

Called hollow wall anchor bolts, these enable a screw to be fixed into a hollow wall or door where a normal screw and wall anchor would have nothing to grip or fit into. The fixing is fitted into a pre-drilled hole and when screwed tight the outer casing folds up against the inner face of the wall or panel to keep the screw firmly in place.

anchor plugs

For a screw to grip securely into masonry, a plug must first be inserted into the hole. Anchor plugs are commonly made of plastic and come in all sizes to suit screws. There are a number of other plugs for use on soft masonry or hollow walls such as wallboard. Threaded plugs screw directly into the wall. Nailable plugs consist of a nail with a plug attached which is hammered into a pre-drilled hole.

knock-down fittings

Fixings required for self-assembly furniture are normally included. They are made specifically for the product so may look different from standard ones. For tightening bolts you may need an Allen wrench. This fits snugly into a hexagonal socket in the head of a bolt and is then turned. These are often supplied with the product, but if not you can buy an inexpensive set of several sizes.

material world

Keep a supply of ingredients for basic jobs, general repairs, and maintenance.

general supplies

Keep small quantities of the following supplies:

sand paper

It is used for smoothing rough surfaces. Available in different grades from coarse- to fine-grit. Some can be used with water for an extra-smooth finish.

patching compound

For filling holes in walls and ceilings. Available in powder form—which is made into a paste by adding water— or ready mixed in a bucket. Although the ready-mixed type is convenient and the right consistency, it is more expensive and hardens if the lid is not put on properly or it is kept for more than a few months.

wood filler

For filling holes in woodwork that is to remain unpainted. Comes as a stiff, ready-made paste in a can and is available in a variety of wood colors.

Electrical tape

Wrap round any wires that may be exposed when changing light fittings.

masking tape

Invaluable for tricky paint jobs such as window casings. Can be used on a drill bit to mark the required depth of a hole or as a guide for straight cutting through pipes and wood.

Teflon tape

Fine, thin tape wound round the threads of screwed plumbing joints to make a good seal and prevent leaks. Useful in place of a washer in emergencies.

penetrating oil

Fine oil is an easy solution to squeaky doors and acts as a lubricant to facilitate unscrewing old hardware. Available in a spray can, it comes with a long thin tube for aiming accurately into deep crevices.

mineral spirits

A solvent for oil-based paints, essential for cleaning paintbrushes and splashes. Also useful for preparing old woodwork for re-painting and removing of greasy stains.

materials

Finding, choosing, and using the right materials is a must:

wood

A pleasing material to work with. It feels and smells good, and is easy to use if you stick to straight lines. It comes in a variety of lengths, widths, and thicknesses. Solid wood comes sawn (rough) or planed (smooth). Ignore the rough stuff. Planed is best for interior jobs: it looks nicer and won't give you so many splinters. Narrow lengths of wood are used for construction purposes, for holding something up, or attaching something. Smaller strips or moldings can be used for decorative and strengthening purposes such as shelf or door lipping. Stronger, chunky sizes are used for frameworks, installing bath tubs, or building interior walls. Wider sections are used as baseboards, fascias, shelving, and floorboards.

Most wood sold for building work is inexpensive softwood. It comes from coniferous, sustainable forests, so you don't need to feel guilty about using it. It has an open grain and can be painted, but also looks nice varnished, waxed, or

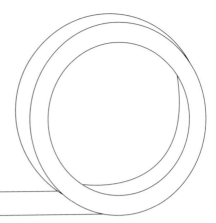

stained. Hardwoods are much more expensive and have denser, more interesting grains. They are used for countertops, furniture, and fancy cabinets. Veneers are very thin slivers of hardwood glued onto reconstituted wood, such as chipboard, particleboard, or plywood. Veneered board has the subtle colors and grains of hardwood without being so expensive, although it is not always a perfect substitute for the real thing. However, it can be practical and is fine for shelving and cabinet door panels.

Manufactured boards are those made from reconstituted wood that has been sliced, ground, or chopped up and then glued together again with bonding agents. They come in various forms including plywood, MDF (medium-density fiberboard), chipboard, and blockboard. Plywood and MDF have a smooth finish suitable for painting and are used for paneling and boxing in; MDF can also be used for doors and furniture. Chipboard has a smooth finish but is very porous so is mostly used as a lightweight base for laminated shelving, countertops, and flooring. All the boards are available in various thicknesses and sizes.

metal

Beginners will use metal in the form of tubing for shower curtains and clothes rails, and copper pipes for simple plumbing jobs. Stainless steel and zinc sheeting can be used for countertops or backsplashes, but is difficult to cut so should be used for straightforward jobs.

plastic

Many plumbing pipes, such as sink, washing machine, and dishwasher waste pipes are all plastic and are easily assembled with no need for adhesives or heat. Plastic conduit is used for concealing exposed electric wiring and plastic edging strip is used for tiling. Plastic sheeting is sometimes used in place of glass for shower screens, picture frames, and other places where glass would be too heavy or constitute a safety hazard. Thicker plastic sheet is not an easy material for amateurs to deal with so get a professional to help with it.

Home improvement stores are full of plastic moldings, ceiling coves, edging strips, decorative panels, and sundry hooks and handles. Most of these will be shunned by style-conscious

shoppers but a few, plain items can be used effectively.

glass

Glass is wonderful stuff, but can also be quite dangerous. You are strongly advised to buy it ready cut to the exact size required. Glaziers will do this for you; they will also polish the edges so that they are neater and safer. As well as its obvious use in windows, doors, and picture frames, glass is frequently used for shelves and shower screens. These will need to be of special toughened safety glass so get it ready cut and finished.

A wide variety of glass is now available, as it is increasingly being used for cool, modern interiors. Wired safety glass is chic as well as sensible and looks very architectural. Etched glass is all the rage; it filters light beautifully and provides privacy. Glass bricks (as used in Modernist houses in the 1920s and '30s) are now very popular again and come in several finishes and colors. They are easy to use and, with care, can look stunning. Mirror glass is available in ready-finished sheets of various sizes with pre-drilled holes for fixing to a wall or door (or even ceiling!).

safety first

The increasing interest in interiors and number of people taking up do-it-yourself jobs has led to a corresponding increase in the number of accidents involving home improvers.

Falling off a ladder is easy, as is slicing fingers, severing arteries, and burning skin. Taking precautions and following instructions is essential for all fun-loving people who value their health and bodies.

Everyone should have a first-aid kit in their home. Make sure it is stocked with all the essentials before embarking on any home improvement task.

As well as the danger of damage from saws, hammers, and drills, other potential hazards to health come from dust, fumes, and chemicals. Paint, paint solvents, varnishes, adhesives, and fillers are all potentially harmful, so it is essential that you follow all manufacturer's instructions and heed all warnings.

labeling

Many products are harmful to the touch and also give off potentially dangerous fumes. Even paint fumes can cause dizziness and mild nausea, so ensure there is plenty of ventilation; open all the windows in the room you are working in, but keep doors closed to prevent the fumes from invading other areas.

ALWAYS read the labels on any product BEFORE opening. Look for the following symbols: Harmful, Toxic, Highly Flammable, and Corrosive.

Harmful

Toxic

Highly Flammable

Corrosive

gloves

Ordinary household rubber gloves will protect against germs and possible skin irritants, but wear longer and thicker rubber gloves when using strong chemicals and corrosives. It is a good idea to wear heavy-duty gloves when handling heavy or rough materials with sharp edges, but be careful they don't get in the way and reduce grip or dexterity.

safety glasses or goggles

Eye damage can be caused by flying sawdust or metal particles, sprays and splashes from paints and other potentially harmful liquids, so have a pair of safety glasses or goggles handy. Don't, however, allow them to increase the risk of injury by impeding your vision for tasks where accuracy is important.

face masks

There is already enough pollution around without subjecting your lungs to yet more noxious substances so wear a mask to protect you from dust and fumes but make sure you get the right mask for the job: DUST For cutting and sanding wood and smoothing down wallboard compound or spackling, use a simple fibrous paper mask. You may look like an extra from Planet of the Apes, but never mind.

FUMES Many of the new products involved in painting, varnishing, and sealing are quick-drying. This is made possible only with the use of sophisticated solvents, some of which give off harmful fumes. The instructions will recommend the use of a respirator mask, which is usually made from molded rubber, formed to fit snugly round the nose and mouth, with an adjustable strap to keep it tight. A special filter fits into a round breathing area. You may sound like the beast from the deep, and look like a storm trooper from Star Wars, but at least you will be conscious. It is important when buying a mask that you get the correct filter for the chemical involved: the instructions on the product will tell you which one, but if in doubt ask an expert or telephone the manufacturer.

ladders

Always make sure the feet of ladders and stepladders are on a level surface. Set a ladder up so the foot is 3 feet away from the base of the wall for every 13 feet of ladder height. If you are scared of heights, get someone to stand at the bottom (or persuade them to do the job for you). Make sure that stepladders are fully unfolded and all four feet are on the ground and level. Don't wear flip-flops or backless footwear when using ladders as you will look silly and probably fall off. Even if you don't, your feet will soon start to hurt, so sturdy shoes or boots are best.

clothing

Scarves, necklaces, and long floaty clothes are potential death-traps. Carefully disarrayed hair looks sexy but those overlong bangs could cause you to make a fatal error, so tie your hair back or bundle it into a nice hat. It's sensible to keep your arms and legs covered to guard against cuts, grazes, and splashes. Wear comfortable footwear that is flexible and preferably covers the whole foot. Tuck in long laces to prevent them getting caught up in machinery or tripping you. You don't have to eschew fashion completely—work clothes are cool anyway—but be aware that paint won't wash out and some products can bleach or even burn holes in clothing.

jobs for the girls
an introduction to core skills

Home improvement jobs encompass everything from knocking a nail into a wall to building an extension with an en-suite bathroom. This chapter will encourage you to use a screw rather than a nail and enable you to put up a snazzy toilet paper holder and a smart shelf in the bathroom, but not how to build it.

Many a nice home has been turned into a realtor's nightmare by overenthusiastic and overconfident people insisting on Doing it Themselves. Home "improvements" can actually ruin a property. It is a wise home handywoman who recognizes her own limitations and sets realistic goals. The shape, size, and style of your home will dictate how much you can or can't do, as well as what you should or shouldn't do. If you have a beautiful house with vast rooms, high ceilings, and wonderful architectural details, then your do-it-yourself activities should be limited to enhancing its inherent characteristics and keeping it in good repair. If you have a small, featureless space, you may add some decoration, and if your living quarters are small, you will probably benefit from a few more shelves. A bit of judicious home improvement can transform cramped into cozy and horrible into rather nice.

Drilling your first hole is one of life's milestones: once you have done it you will probably want to do it again. In fact, if you want to put up anything more complex than a single, small hook you will need to drill several holes. Getting those holes in the right place will ensure everything is straight and on the level. Possession of a power drill will increase your power base and propel you toward bigger and better things. Once you have learned to attach a simple strip of wood to a wall the world of home improvement will open up before you.

Even apparently complex jobs such as putting in a new kitchen often involves nothing more than drilling holes and putting in screws. Making the holes and getting them in exactly the right place is not always as easy as it sounds, but then again it's not rocket science. With patience, practice, and an understanding of the principles of wall construction, it is perfectly possible for amateurs to produce professional-looking work.

Mastering these basics skills won't turn you into a professional but will enable you to carry out simple jobs that will turn your home into a more convenient, functional, and stylish place. Once you have the confidence to take on the simpler tasks it is often a relatively small step to the more ambitious projects. On the other hand, knowing what is involved in Doing it Yourself may be enough to make you decide to stick to the easy stuff—and feel much better about paying someone else do the big jobs.

the hole story

Many home improvement jobs involve attaching things to walls, and to do this you will almost certainly have to make some holes. But before drilling into any walls, floors, or ceilings it is very important to find out where electricity cables, gas or water pipes are and take care to avoid them. The consequences of drilling into any of these could be death and disaster. Don't drill near electrical outlets or immediately above, below, and around light switches or light fittings. Various inexpensive, battery-powered devices are available which light up to indicate the presence of metal pipework in walls or under floors. Similar instruments are also available to detect the position of electrical cables.

size matters

A drilled hole is usually made for a screw, the most common form of fixing. It is almost impossible to screw directly into plaster, concrete, or brick so you will need to use a power drill and masonry bit. The depth and diameter of the hole will depend on the size of the screw and length of the wall anchor you are using. A certain amount of dust and debris will collect at the far end of the hole so you need to drill a little deeper than the length of the anchor plug. To ensure the hole is the right size, wrap a piece of tape around the drill bit to mark the depth required or use an "adjustable depth stop" which is sometimes supplied with a power drill.

off the wall

Walls are not necessarily straightforward. If they are made from plaster on brick or blockwork you should be able to drill a hole in them fairly easily with a standard power drill, but if they are made from concrete you will need one with more power. Tools can always be rented so you don't need to spend a vast amount of money on expensive equipment. Soft walls can also be a problem as a small hole can easily turn into a large chasm, so you may need to use threaded wall anchors. Hollow wall anchor bolts can be used on hollow partition walls (see page 15), but you will need to be careful as hollow walls may be unsuitable for items that are heavy or structures that are load-bearing.

on the ceiling

Drilling into ceilings can be unwise and the best advice to novices is not to do it. The certain presence of electric wires and possibly water pipes, plus the fact that they are not usually solid, makes it a risky business.

Ceilings usually consist of drywall panels nailed to wooden joists (supporting beams) and then plastered. In old houses the ceiling plaster was applied to thin strips of wood known as laths. The plaster on an old ceiling may be thick enough to accommodate a fairly deep hole and, for newer ceilings, a threaded fixing can be used on wallboard. However, if you want to hang something heavy you will have to find a joist so you have something solid to screw into. Finding one is not always easy but you try tapping along the ceiling until you find an area that doesn't sound hollow. If this area extends right across the ceiling then you can be pretty confident you have found a joist. Some ceilings in apartments are solid concrete and are difficult to drill into.

screwed up

Screws can be fixed easily into most wood so a deep, pre-drilled hole is unnecessary. However, the screw will go in easily and more accurately if there is a narrow hole to start it off and guide it in; this is called a pilot hole. You can make one using a drill with a fine bit or a bradawl. If you are putting up hooks or fixings that have a screw thread attached, they will also be easier to screw in, and will go in straighter, if you drill pilot holes first. Nails don't normally need a pilot hole, but if they are very long, or the wood very thick, they will benefit from being helped on their way via a pilot hole. This will also reduce the risk of the nail bending, going in at the wrong angle, or splitting the wood.

When a piece of wood is being screwed onto something else—another piece of wood or a wall, for example—it is a good idea to drill a clearance hole for the screw. Drill right through the first piece of wood so that you can use a bradawl to mark the position on the other piece of wood or the wall. If you are screwing into wood and don't want the head of the screw to show, then you will need to countersink the screw. This involves drilling a shallow crater (using a countersink) at the top of the drilled pilot hole so that the screwhead disappears. This crater can then be filled with wood filler to give a smooth surface.

drill call

Making holes in materials other than masonry and wood can be tricky. When drilling into ceramic tiles—putting up a shower attachment or towel rail, for example—care is needed to avoid cracking or chipping. Stick a piece of masking tape to the surface of the tile to help steady the drill bit and stop it slithering and shooting off across the tile. Use a masonry bit but set the drill to rotary action—hammer action will damage the tile—and use a slow speed.

Similarly, when drilling into metal make a small dent with a nail punch, or a bradawl if it is fairly soft, and place the V-shaped end of the metal bit into this dent before starting to drill. If you have to drill through plastic-coated laminated boards always drill downward through the top of the surface: drilling upward from below can cause the laminate to crack.

drilling a hole

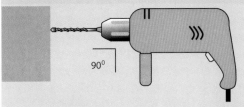

Check that there are no wires or pipes in the wall. Mark where you want the center of the hole to be. Place the point of the drill bit firmly on this mark, at a 90-degree angle to the wall.

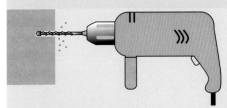

Turn on the drill. Keeping it as level and straight as possible, push the drill bit gently into the wall. Continue pushing until the hole is drilled to the depth required.

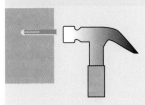

Insert a wall anchor plug in the drilled hole and tap gently into place with a hammer.

To fix your hardware (such as a coat hook), place it against the wall so the screw hole and anchor line up, insert the screw, hold firmly in place, and tighten with a screwdriver.

on the level

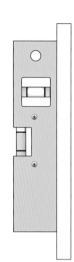

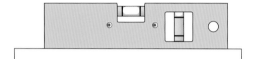

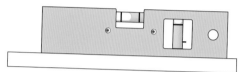

For any job to be done well, accurate measurements must be made. This involves measuring spaces, lengths, heights, depths, amounts, and angles. Marking things is also important, whether it is a small dot for a screw, a straight line for cutting along, or more complicated marks on walls for lining up against. Getting things straight, parallel, and level is a vital part of getting things to look right and fit together properly. This involves tape measures, try squares, swinging plumb boblines, and delving into the spirit level world.

straight talking

Be warned: walls, floors, and ceilings are never perfectly flat nor perfectly straight. Perfect right angles rarely exist between walls, floors, and ceilings so don't assume the measurements at both ends of a room will be the same. Alcoves are particularly prone to inconsistent measurements so always measure across the back as well as across the gap at the front, and take measurements at intervals all the way down.

When drawing dots or lines to mark the position of fixings, always use a carpenter's level to make sure they are parallel and straight. Don't rely on your "eye" and don't take measurements up from the floor or down from the ceiling for the reasons just mentioned. For long distances, use a yardstick or ruler and a length of wood as a guide, but always in conjunction with a level as wood is never perfectly straight and may have a bend in it. A plumb bob—which consists of a heavy weight on the end of a long length of string—will automatically create a vertical when allowed to hang free from a nail at the top of a wall and is often used for marking guidelines for wallpaper. However, this really needs two people— one to hold the plumb bob in place and the other to draw the guidelines—so it may be easier to stick to a level and a straightedge. To stop the plumb bob swinging, place the weighted end in a bucket of water.

When taking a measurement always keep the tape measure straight and level— even a very slight angle will affect accuracy. To mark a length of wood for cutting, put a small pencil mark on the edge against the required measurement. If the wood is narrow, use a try square to draw a line right across. For wider pieces, measure along both sides and join up the dots. To ensure accuracy for longer cuts, mark the measurement in the middle as well as the edges, then join up the three dots.

making your mark

Marking panels will require extra care to ensure accuracy. Use as many of the finished edges of the material as possible, as cutting a perfect right angle is difficult. Mark the measurements at frequent intervals and use a long straightedge such as a metal ruler to draw the lines. Check right angles with a try square or a framing square. Better still, get it cut to size at the lumberyard or home improvement store.

When putting up a small item, such as a small shelf, where two or more screws are required, it is a good idea to mark and drill just one hole to start with. Once the first hole has been made, put up the item using a single screw and then, using a level, mark the positions of the other holes. Remove the first screw and the item before drilling the other holes.

cutting edge

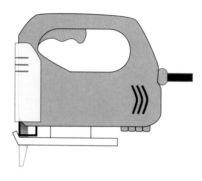
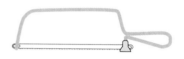

Unless you are very canny, you will not be able to avoid cutting something at sometime. Cutting usually involves a little danger, but with a modest selection of tools and a few good tips, you can cut perfectly straight lines in wood, metal, plastic, and tiles and still have all digits intact. "Measure twice, cut once" should be your mantra. In the excitement of creativity it is easy to misread a measurement and the resulting mistakes can be costly as well as extremely irritating.

The quality of a cut dictates the quality of the finished job. Just as a bad haircut detracts from a stunning outfit, so a bad carpentry cut ruins a classy interior. While you may consider trimming your friend's bangs, you probably wouldn't attempt a full haircut; likewise if a home improvement job involves sophisticated cuts get someone else to do it.

wood cuts

Wood is fairly easy to cut with a suitable, sharp saw. In order to achieve a clean, straight cut it is necessary to coordinate hand with eye, and have an affinity with the third dimension. As well as controlling the saw so it keeps to a straight line, you must make sure the blade is cutting down at an angle of 90 degrees—if not you will end up with an angled cut that does not look very good and will cause fitting problems.

Short cuts—such as sawing a length from a narrow piece of wood—are not too difficult but a longer cut requires more skill or a specific tool to produce a neat finish. Keeping straight is not easy for beginners, but it helps if you have a sharp cutting tool and something to hold the material firmly. There are several workbenches on the market. Although the name may conjure up images of huge structures made from great slabs of wood, the simplest version consists of two lengths of wood on top of a metal frame and the whole thing folds up for easy storage. As well as providing a surface for working, a vise mechanism allows you to clamp a piece of wood or other material between the two lengths of wood to hold it firmly in place for easier cutting, drilling, and sanding.

saw points

Make sure anything to be cut is on a level surface and held securely by clamps or a vise. To cut with a handsaw, start by placing the upper part of the saw blade (the bit near the handle) on the marked spot on the edge of the wood. Then dig the blade gently into the wood and draw it backward a little way to cut a small nick. Using the nick to locate the saw blade—making sure that it is vertical and is lined up with the cutting line—start sawing by pushing the blade forward and pulling it backward.

To begin with you may find the saw sticks and you have to keep restarting, but once you get into a regular rhythm try not to stop until you have cut through. Keep an eye on the cutting line to make sure you are maintaining a straight line: you will find that a sprinkling of sawdust obscures it from view and you have to blow it away at frequent intervals. If your cut is deviating wildly from its prescribed path, then stop and try straightening up by repositioning the blade. Ragged cuts can always be smoothed with sand paper.

Alternatively, use a power jigsaw. Most modern models will make straight and curved cuts in wood up to approximately $2^{3}/_{4}$ inches thick and metal up to $^{1}/_{4}$ inch thick, as well as most plastics. Variable speed allows you to slow down for intricate cuts and a

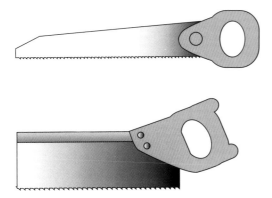

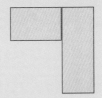

A simple butt joint as used for support boards on walls.

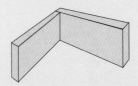

Plain baseboards can be joined using a simple butt joint.

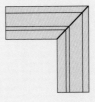

A mitered joint as used on the moldings around a door or a picture frame.

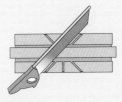

A miter block for use with narrow strips of wood. 45-degree slots are used to cut accurate mitered joints.

dustblower keeps the cutting line visible; some jigsaws even extract the dust as you go. Various other features help keep all edges straight. A base plate helps to keep the drill vertical for straight lines and features are incorporated for cutting curves and beveled edges.

Circular power saws are bigger than power jigsaws and are only really worth buying or renting if you are cutting a lot of panels or are using very thick wood.

cut down to size

Whatever you use, beginners will find that any cut longer than about 6 inches is likely to produce a less-than-perfect edge. This is okay if it isn't going to show, but for shelves, countertops, panels used for boxing in pipes, or doors a neat edge is essential.

A machined edge is best and the bigger the machine the better. Many home improvement stores have such machines and will cut wood (straight cuts only) to your precise measurements. The service is usually inexpensive; sometimes the first few cuts are free and then the charge kicks in. Before you go to buy wood find out the dimensions of standard lengths and widths so that you can work out the most economical way of getting the sizes you need. Work out exactly what you need and write down all the measurements with diagrams as well. Load the uncut lengths into your shopping cart and take them, and the diagrams with all the correct measurements, to the cutting service area. Sometimes these services are much in demand and lines build up, so don't ask for too much at one time. Try to go at less busy times and telephone first to make sure the cutting service is available.

a word about joints

The simplest way to join two pieces of wood together is with a butt joint, where two edges are butted together and secured with nails, screws, or wood glue. This is fine when the joint is to be covered up or painted, but for a job such as putting new frame around a door or wooden quadrant around a floor edge a mitered joint is necessary for a neater finish. This involves cutting an accurate 45-degree angle which can be constructed using a protractor or, for narrow pieces of wood, a miter block.

cutting remarks

Wherever and whenever possible home improvement virgins should stick to straight lines. Negotiating corners, curves and pipes can turn simple jobs into lengthy procedures so think hard before trying to fit your way around them.

Cutting out slots for a single pipe or straight-sided object is okay, as you can cut a straight-sided slot to accommodate them. However, this is not quite as straightforward as it sounds. Making the two cuts which form either side of the cutout is simple, but it is impossible to cut the third side with a conventional saw as there is never enough room for the blade.

cut it out

If the indent is not very deep you can use a coping saw—a frame saw with a very thin, removable blade—that can be passed through a drilled hole at one corner of the cut and then reattached. In theory, you should then be able to cut along the other edge and the blade swivels to allow you to cut out holes and curves. This is not easy, however, and can only be used for thin wood.

Cutting a chunk out of a countertop is more difficult; you would have to use a jigsaw, drilling large holes in the corner to allow the blade to fit through. Slots for slim pipes are more straightforward, as you can drill a hole slightly larger than the pipe, then cut in from the edge to meet the hole forming a round ended slot that will fit snugly around the pipe. Beginners often end up with a less-than-neat fit, so unless you are confident you can do a good job don't risk messing up expensive materials.

on edge

It can be difficult to get a neat edge when cutting through wood strip flooring as the plastic coating is brittle. To minimize damage, always cut with the top surface faceup when using a power saw or when using a jigsaw, which cuts on the upstroke, cut with the "top" surface facing downward. Alternatively, get it cut in your home improvement store.

Plastic edgings and pipes are easy enough to cut but cutting plastic sheets is more difficult. Soft plastic can clog saw teeth and thicker, rigid sheets will crack unless it is cut carefully. Very thick plastic sheets are also expensive so get them cut professionally.

hacked off

Cutting metal is easier than it sounds, but to begin with it is best to avoid sheet metal or heavy metal hardware.

Many home improvements involve cutting metal tubes used for curtain rods, clothes rails, and pipe plumbing. A small hacksaw with a thin, replaceable blade is adequate for this, but it can be difficult to control as the blade is also quite flexible.

A piece of tape stuck around the tube as a guide will help you to see if you are cutting at 90 degrees, but an easier option is to use a pipe cutter. This is an ingenious device which holds the pipe in place while a small blade, tightened by a hand-turned screw, makes a neat, straight cut. Cutting metal produces a lot of heat, so don't touch the edges of the metal or the saw until things have cooled down. Smooth ragged edges with a file or sand paper but be careful not to cut your fingers on any sharp metal.

To cut through thick metal, ceramic, or stone it will be necessary to use a special power tool that has a tough, circular blade which whizzes around fast enough to cut through very hard materials. This tool is not expensive and

cutting around
a pipe

looks manageable, but the effort needed and the noise and dust generated during its use means it is more suited to professionals than beginners.

Special cutters can be bought for making clean, straight cuts in ceramic tiles, but for awkward shapes you will need to use a tile nipper, a tool that takes a certain amount of skill to use.

Pliers with a cutting blade are available for cutting electric cables and wires, and some have a little notch for stripping off the plastic coating on wires when making connections.

Utility knives can be used for cutting paper, vinyl, carpeting, and thin plastic. The chunky ones with replaceable blades are versatile as a variety of blades are available including curved ones for cutting carpeting, and a small saw blade.

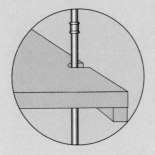

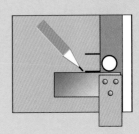

1. Mark the cutting lines on each side of pipe.

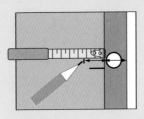

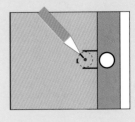

2. Measure the distance from the wall to the front of the pipe and mark on the shelf or countertop.

3. Mark the center of the hole to be drilled for positioning the drill bit.

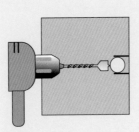

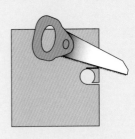

4. Drill out hole using a power drill and a large bit.

5. Cut along the marked lines using a saw.

Many home improvement jobs involve attaching things to walls, fixing things to other things, and joining things together. Most things are secured by means of screw, nail, bolt, glue or, occasionally, double-sided tape. The method of fixing depends on several factors including function, materials involved, size of components, load-bearing requirements, practicality, and aesthetic considerations.

The simplest fixing is a nail knocked into a wall and, unsophisticated though this is, it is perfectly okay for hanging small pictures and other lightweight objects. A screw will do the same job but will be stronger.

Some items such as hooks, toilet-roll, and soap holders are secured directly to a wall with screws. Shelves, towel rails, shades, and curtain rods are attached using special fixings, brackets, or boards that are screwed on first.

It is essential that the correct type and size of fixing is used, and that they are secured firmly into the wall, ceiling, or window casing. Shelves, cabinets, shades, and curtain rods are often required to support a considerable amount

of weight as well as being subjected to constant pressure and movement.

fixed assets

When buying fixtures you will find that screws and wall anchors are often provided; this is useful but check they are suitable for the material they are to be screwed into. To get screws to stay in walls you must provide something for the screw to grip onto. Simple plastic wall anchors are usually sufficient for masonry walls but, as discussed in the section on making holes (see pages 22–3), soft or hollow walls will need special fixings. If you want to fix something heavy to a partition wall you will need to locate the solid wood support and screw into that. As with ceilings, finding that support may be a matter of tapping until the hollow sound stops, then trying a screw to see if it digs into something solid.

Other home improvement jobs involve covering things up. Permanent panels, as used for boxing in pipes or covering unsightly features, can be made from particleboard, plywood, or solid wood. They are fixed to a wooden framework using brads which are very thin and will be

virtually invisible. Where panels need to be removed for access to plumbing or electricity, you will need to use screws, and if the panel is visible use mirror screws.

Baseboards are often nailed directly to the wall with long masonry nails, but it is kinder to the wall, the wood, and possibly your fingers, if you use screws. Window and door trims are thinner and usually have a molded profile that makes them unsuitable for screws, therefore they are usually nailed in place with thin brads.

stick 'em up

Modern adhesives are very efficient and some are strong enough to be used instead of nails or screws. They can be useful for poor-quality or hollow walls that are unsuitable for screws or nails, or in places or situations (an awkward corner or proximity to wiring or pipework for example) where putting in a nail or screw could be difficult or even dangerous. However, positioning must be accurate and it is not easy handling and maneuvering long lengths of wood coated in quick-drying adhesive. Also, bear in mind that anything stuck down will be difficult to remove without damag-

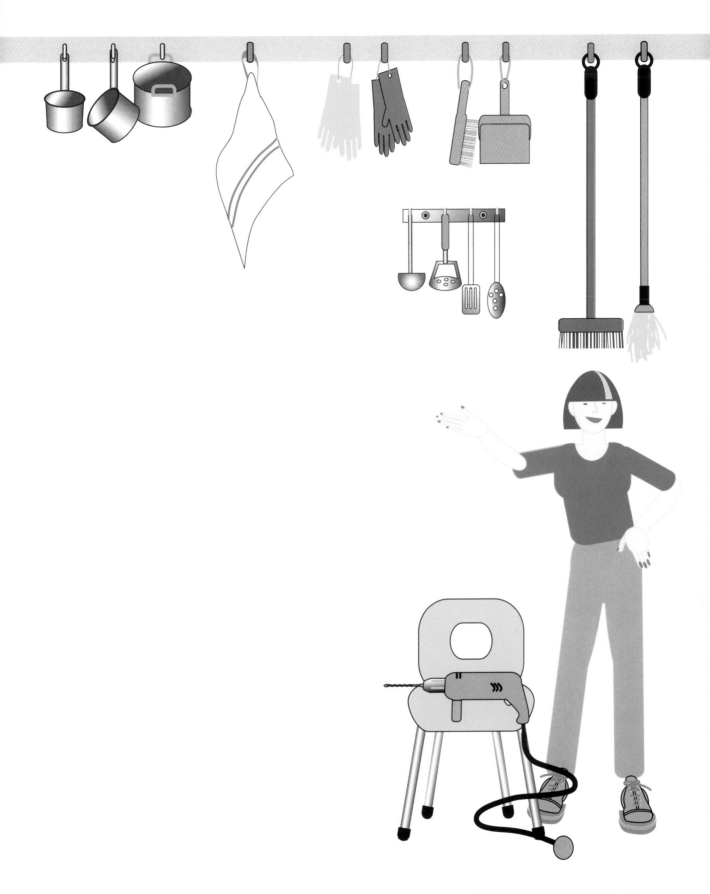

put-up jobs

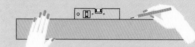

1. Cut the length of board required, hold it in position using a level to ensure that it is level, and draw a line with a pencil across the top. Mark the position of the ends.

2 and 3. Take down the board and place on a work surface. Mark the position of the screws, making sure they are evenly spaced. Drill through the board using a twist drill.

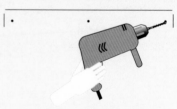

4 and 5. Place the board against the wall and make an indented mark using a bradawl. Make holes in the wall using a power drill and pop a walll anchor into each hole.

6. Fix the battening to the wall using screws which go right through the board and into the wall anchors.

One of the most useful things to screw on a wall is a support board to which other items, such as hooks, shelves, countertops, cabinets, and the like, can be fixed. Putting up a support board is a passport to greater things and once you have done it you will feel you have earned a certain amount of handywoman credibility.

Support boards are widely available. Although their dimensions vary according to the job, the most commonly used size is what builders refer to as "two-by-one," which means 2 inches wide by 1 inch thick. What the board is to be used for will dictate its length, position-ing, and how you treat the ends, but whatever its size the method of putting it up remains the same.

putting up a support board

1. Cut the board to the length required. Hold it in position against the wall, using a level to ensure that it is perfectly horizontal, then draw a pencil line on the wall across the top of the board. Mark the position of the ends.

2. Take down the board from the wall and place it on a workbench or work table. Along the center of the board mark the position of the screws with a bradawl, making sure there is no more than approximately 20 inches between each one and placing the end screws not more than 1 $\frac{1}{2}$ inches from the edge.

3. Using a twist drill that is slightly thinner than the screws, make holes right through the board at the marked positions (but make sure you don't drill into the work-bench or your best table).

4. Hold the board firmly in position against the wall along the pencil lines. Poke a bradawl through each drilled hole to make an indented mark on the wall.

5. Take down the board from the wall again and using a power drill make holes in the wall on these indented markings. Pop a wall anchor into each drilled hole in the wall.

6. Fix the support board to the wall using screws that are long enough to go right through it and tighten in the wall anchors in the wall.

7. Perfectionists will suggest countersinking all the screwholes into the board, but modern softwoods are usually soft enough to allow you to screw a little tighter so that the screwhead embeds itself in the wood. You can then put wood filler over the top of the screwheads to hide them and achieve a smooth finish.

uses for support boards

Putting up a support board allows a long length of wood to be fixed to the wall using a relatively small number of screws. It provides a strong base and suitable material for attaching fixings such as nails, brads, screws, and hooks and therefore is used for several jobs around the home.

Shelves and countertops are supported by boards that are fixed to walls. It is also used as a framework for boxing in pipes or putting up wall paneling. A support board can be fixed to a wall for hanging heavy weights such as a wallhanging or a large picture and can also be useful on a hollow wall where the board can be fixed securely to solid wood studs.

Roman blinds are hung from support boards and other types of shades or shutters are often attached to a wood strip rather than the wall or ceiling. Wood is easier to screw into than walls so it makes sense to put up a length of wood using a small number of long, strong screws and use this for screwing hooks or fittings into. Lighting and curtain fixtures can be concealed behind a wooden fascia attached to a wood strip. Some home improvement jobs involve putting up a temporary level support board or ledger, as a guide against which to line up tiles or kitchen units.

Sort out your music collection by putting up a wall-mounted CD rack.

Make sure you're never caught again by installing new bathroom fixtures, including a toilet-roll holder.

Make a coat rack by screwing a row of simple hooks to a support board fixed to the wall.

Keep your bathroom tidy by hanging a new medicine cabinet, complete with mirror for those essential make-up checks.

Avoid those last-minute searches for your house or car keys by putting up a hook inside the front door.

Decorate your walls by hanging that heavy picture frame or mirror at last.

fix it

common repair jobs around your home

Keeping your home in good order is the grown-up equivalent of tidying your bedroom, but though the task seems uninviting and rather daunting, as soon as you've done it you wish you'd made the effort sooner. If you own your home it makes good sense to look after it in order to maintain its value and keep it a desirable property should you wish to sell. But the best reasons for fixing that loose floorboard or squeaky door is that your home will be a much nicer, and possibly safer, place to live in. Major works such as replastering walls and ceilings or laying new floors should definitely be left to the skilled professionals, but repairing holes is as easy as pie and putting on new baseboards is not too difficult (but getting the old baseboards off can be tricky).

Floors have a big impact on your home, so don't be afraid to rip up tired, worn out floorcoverings. If your home is old and you are very lucky you could find a beautiful wooden or tiled floor beneath which you can clean and restore. If not, ordinary floorboards can be sanded and sealed for the fashionable bare look. Concrete is cool and can be painted or sealed for the chic, industrial style.

Walls and ceilings cannot be ignored, and will attract unwelcome attention if they are marked and dented. However, some judicious home improvement can make them melt into the background or stand out boldly, whichever you prefer. Although open plan is all the rage and walls are out of favor, novices are strongly advised to leave walls alone except for patching them up and decorating. Walls play a very important role supporting ceilings, upper floors, roofs, and even whole buildings, so don't even think of removing one—the consequences could be disastrous. If you want to open up your space, get a qualified architect or engineer to advise on how best to do it.

Removing a door will open up a space and is not difficult, and neither is hanging a new one. Getting a door to fit well may be a little more complicated but is definitely not beyond beginners. Windows are trickier as they form part of the structure of a building, but getting them to open or shut smoothly is straightforward enough. New hardware such as window and door catches will not only work better, but look good, too, just as a dull cabinet or door will be transformed by new handles and knobs.

Fixing and repairing are also part of the essential preparation work for painting and decorating, so once your home is looking good it makes sense to ensure that it is safe and secure. Smoke alarms are inexpensive and can save lives, while a variety of locks and bolts are available that are both discreet and easy to attach to doors and windows to make them intruder-proof without making your home look, and feel, like a fortress.

things to know about floors

An unattractive floor will detract from even the sleekest furniture and decor so it is worth investing time and money in this important area. The choice of flooring will depend on your personal preferences and circumstances, but even on a small budget it is possible to produce a great-looking base to complement and enhance your interior.

bare is beautiful

... especially if it is limestone, old waxed boards, polished concrete, or brand new solid wood. Ordinary floorboards can look good when sanded, painted, varnished, or waxed. Old tiles, flagstone, and even concrete can look beautiful if cleaned up and sealed.

cold feet

Hard floors, particularly concrete or ceramic tiles, can be cold, especially in winter when they can defy even the best heating system. Necessary ventilation under wooden floors can become an undesirable draft around ankles if the gaps are too wide.

quiet please

Your downstairs neighbors may also be pleased at the return of carpeting. Bare floors are noisy, particularly hard materials such as tiles that don't absorb any sound. Tiling an entire ground floor may look stunning but will have the intimate ambience of the local swimming pool.

floors matter

The subtlest colors and the chicest furniture will never look any good if your floor is unsightly. Light-colored floors make an interior seem larger and using the same floor finish throughout will make it look bigger still.

warm toes

Carpeting is making a comeback and area rugs are all the rage, which is good news for those who have been longing to pad around in comfort and wish to use the floor for activities other than walking on. But if you can't live with clutter, under-floor heating to warm bare floors is now easier and less expensive than ever before.

health matters

Natural materials are kinder to our bodies as well as the environment, so wherever possible stick to wood, natural fibers, and additive-free finishes. Asthma sufferers are often advised to avoid wall-to-wall carpeting but check that your alternative floorcoverings, laminated strip flooring, and any adhesives are free from potentially harmful chemicals.

repairing wooden floors

Replacing a floorboard can either be a simple or rather complicated task depending on its length, width, and accessibility. If you have a beautiful old floor, you may want to get a professional carpenter to treat its repair with the care and respect it deserves.

A short length of floorboard in the middle of a room is relatively easy to deal with, but when faced with long boards and edges the job becomes much more difficult. Unless the floorboard is very damaged or unsightly—or decaying or infested—it is better to rely on sanding and finishing to make it look okay.

Floorboards come in a variety of widths and thicknesses. Inexpensive softwood boards, laid as a base rather than a feature, are usually narrow and of a standard width available from lumber yards and home improvement stores. Old floorboards are often wider, so you may have to go to a salvage yard to find a replacement; it may need cleaning before use.

Floorboards are attached to joists, the chunky lengths of wood that form the framework of the floor (and, in upstairs rooms, support the ceiling below). The floorboards run in the opposite direction to the joists and are normally attached with floor nails that have straight sides to minimize splitting and a narrow, one-sided head that sinks into the wood.

replacing a floorboard

Lifting a floorboard should be done with care to avoid damaging those next to it. Ideally you should use a brick chisel, which has a wide flat blade, for levering up, and a cold chisel which is strong and long enough to insert under the board to

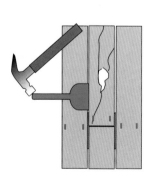

1. Tap the brick chisel into the gap near to the end of the board to be removed. Lever gently until the board begins to lift and the nails start to come out.

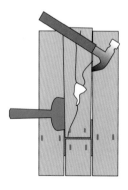

2. Repeat this process at the other end. Insert the claw of a hammer under the lifted board until there is room to insert the cold chisel.

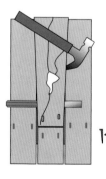

3. Slide the cold chisel underneath the floorboard toward the next set of nails. Repeat this process along the length of the board until it eases out.

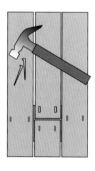

4. Fit the new board into position and nail it down to the joist using floorboard nails. Nail at the ends and wherever it crosses a joist.

assist the levering process. Other useful tools include a claw hammer, floorboard saw, nail set, and floorboard nails.

potential pitfalls

If any of the following apply, you may want to seek help from a carpenter or simply decide not to bother:

Problem: The floorboard edge sits under the baseboard: you will have to lift it up in order to pull it out. If it is a long board that extends under two baseboards, you will have to cut it in half.

Problem: The floorboard is nailed underneath the baseboard: you will have to cut it as close to the baseboard as possible using a floorboard saw.

Problem: The floorboards are tongued and grooved: there is no gap for easy levering.

Problem: The new floorboard sits below the rest of the floor: you will have to put packing underneath (cardboard, Masonite, or thin wood will do) where it is nailed to the joists.

Problem: The new floorboard stands above the rest of the floor: you will either have to make the board thinner by planing or cut a recess into the joists to slot the board into.

rejuvenating wooden floors

Bare wooden floors are popular as they give a fresh, modern look to any interior and can be achieved fairly easily and cheaply by sanding and sealing existing floorboards. The condition of the boards will dictate just how easy this is going to be, but as long as they are sound, the surface isn't too uneven, and there aren't too many holes it shouldn't be too much of a problem.

Sanding does create a lot of dust and noise, however, so warn your neighbors. If you already have polished floorboards in good condition but feel they are a bit dull or dark, think hard before doing any drastic sanding. Cleaning and rewaxing will lighten them and restore them to a glory you didn't know they had. Solid wood parquet floors should be left to the experts; don't risk spoiling them with poorly executed treatments.

on board

If your home is new or recently converted, you may find the boards beneath thefloorcovering have been left in their original, unfinished state. Often they are covered with paint and plaster splashes; if these can't be removed easily by scrubbing and a little paint stripper, you will need to sand them. Old floorboards that are very dirty or are buried beneath many layers of paint or varnish will need a thorough sanding to achieve an even finish.

Badly damaged boards should be replaced. Whether you do this yourself depends on the number of boards involved, their position and size (see panel on replacing a board, pages 38–9). Big gaps between the boards are an aesthetic issue as much as anything, although drafts could also be a problem. If all the gaps are very wide, then either cover them up again or have the floor professionally relaid.

unwelcome guests

If you find evidence of insect infestation in your floorboards, you must check whether it is ongoing. Your floorboards and the joists under them may need to be treated. Get a reputable company to do this unpleasant job for you; after inspection and treatment they will provide a guarantee that is valid for several years, which you will need as proof of treatment for any future buyers of your home.

sanding a wooden floor

Secure any obviously loose floorboards and use a nail set to knock nail heads below the surface; any protruding nails will damage the sanding belt. Remove all furniture, curtains, etc. and open all the windows. Seal gaps around the door with tape and wedge newspaper at the bottom. Hanging a wet sheet on the outside of the door will also help prevent the dust escaping.

You will need to rent a drum sander for the main floor area and an edge sander for the sides and corners. The rental store will give you full operating instructions, including how to change the sanding belt.

You should know that a sander won't necessarily behave as you would expect it to. It will make its own way across the floor without much assistance and must be held back to ensure progress is slow and steady. Don't let go or it will run away. Hold the drum off the floor when you switch it on and lower it gently to begin sanding. Once switched on, it is

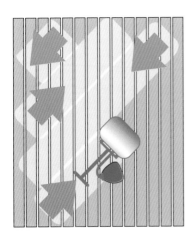

1. Using a coarse-grit sand paper, sand the floor diagonally.

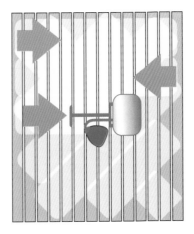

2. Change to a medium-grit paper and sand across the boards.

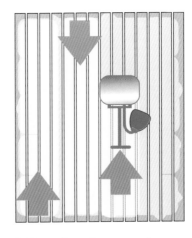

3. Using a fine-grit paper, sand up and down until the surface is smooth.

essential to keep moving: allowing the sander to stay in one spot for any length of time will result in a smooth, but unwanted, hollow in the floor.

You will need to wear a safety dust mask, safety goggles, and ear protection when sanding, as the noise of the sander and the dust from old paint and varnish can be hazardous. Several sandings will be necessary, starting with a coarse-grit sand paper to level the floorboards. For this first sanding, move diagonally across the room, tilting the machine to change direction and overlapping each run to ensure the whole surface is covered. When you have covered the whole floor switch off, sweep up the dust, and then start again, this time sanding diagonally in the other direction. When the floor is flat, change to medium-grit sand paper and continue sanding across the boards. Finally, finish with fine-grit sand paper up and down the boards for a smooth, scratch-free surface. After each stage, repeat the process around the sides and in corners using the edge sander. Use a scraper, a flexible orbital sander, or steel wool to get right up to the baseboards and into the corners. When you have

finished, vacuum the floor, then wipe over the floorboards with a cloth dampened with mineral spirits ready for finishing.

finishing a wooden floor

Be careful not to stain your newly stripped floor. Unfinished wood is porous and absorbs dirt and spills making it difficult to clean. If you need to walk on it, wear clean socks rather than bare feet (as sweat contains substances best kept off absorbent wood) and don't wait too long before applying wood sealer.

Sealing involves reducing the porosity of the surface and/or the creation of a coating that will prevent the penetration of dirt while providing a cleanable surface. What you use depends on the look you want plus practical considerations such as use and amount of wear. There is the usual bewildering array of products on the market, with new, improved versions appearing all the time. Sealers roughly divide into varnishes (which form a hard protective coating) and oils (which soak into the wood and are often finished with an application of wax). Varnish can be applied directly onto new or newly finished wood and, depending on the product, will

need two or more coats to form a hard, durable surface. Choose between a shiny or flat finish. Sanding by hand between coats will give a better result. Finishing oils soak into wood and plump up the wood fibers. Modern versions have additives to help form a waterproof and more dirtproof surface. Waxing on top of these will produce a soft, mellow finish that will, with diligent application, mature well.

For less than perfect wood, a darker finish will disguise a multitude of sins. Avoid using wood stains as it can be difficult to achieve an even finish, instead use a colored wood varnish. Most of these varnishes are available in different wood finishes and using a dark color will achieve a similar effect to a wood stain with less hassle.

If your floorboards are just not good enough to be seen in their natural state, you can always paint them. For a fresh modern look, choose white or gray gloss or floor paint. Applying a wood primer and undercoat first will ensure a smooth, dense finish. A softer effect can be achieved by painting the floor with water-based latex paint and adding a dirtproof coating of clear varnish.

other floor surfaces

Wooden floorboards may be popular but they are not always desirable or practical. Many people prefer the warmth and look of carpeting bare boards. It is often cheaper and easier to carpet a room than re-finish floorboards.

You will be offered a professional laying service when buying carpeting; although it seems expensive it is worth the money. Carpeting is heavy and comes in generous widths making it difficult to handle. Fitting it around features and getting it neatly into corners is not easy. Badly laid carpet will never look good. However, if finances are tight and you are desperate to cheer up a small room then take it on, but avoid expensive thick carpeting and opt for thinner foam-backed carpeting.

In modern homes chipboard is often used in place of floorboards as it is intended to be covered. Although lacking the character of floorboards, chipboard is draft-free and perfectly flat. The joints are usually invisible, so if you want the bare floor look this is a good surface for painting or even sealing with varnish if their color and finish is even.

Old houses, especially those in the country, sometimes have stone floors. Stone or slate slabs are full of character and add a sense of history, but they can also look stunning when used as part of a pared-down, modern interior. Damaged or pitted surfaces are part of the character (call them "distressed" and you will see them in a different way) so don't be put off by any gaps or discoloring. Scrape off any old dirt or paint and give the floor a good scrub using soap and water or, if it is very bad, a special stone cleaner (available from your home improvement store or floor specialist). Fill any gaps using cement-based exterior patching compound; this is available in handy-sized amounts. Just add water, but don't make it too sloppy. It stays workable for about 20 minutes so work it into the gaps, smooth the surface, and wipe excess from surrounding areas. Finish with an appropriate sealer that will soak into the stone preventing dirt penetration. For advice, try calling your local stone floor specialist: they love their subject and will usually be happy to dispense helpful information and suggestions for treatments, products, and so on.

Tiled floors are often found in old homes. Some are decorative, such as the encaustic tiles used in the halls of Victorian and Edwardian houses, while others are plainer and more prosaic, like the quarry tiles found in kitchens and less grand homes. Again, if their condition is not great they may respond to a good clean, regrouting, and sealing (see pages 84–5). Missing tiles can be replaced; you may find a match in an architectural salvage yard. The small spaces left by incomplete or missing mosaic tiles can be filled and, if you are feeling clever, painted to match.

Consider freshening up a modern ceramic tiled floor by regrouting, perhaps with a new color. Damaged tiles can be removed so that a new one can be fitted into the space (wear safety glasses for this job).

Of course, you may just have a boring old concrete floor, but if you are keen on the brutal industrial look you can patch it up and either paint it or just seal it. Clean out holes and cracks, removing any loose material, then get rid of all the dust (with a vacuum cleaner). Fill the gaps using cement-based exterior patching compound as above. Concrete is dusty, so you will have to seal it if it is to be left uncovered.

wood strip flooring

Wood strip flooring comes in a range of lengths, widths, materials, and prices. Planks or sections fit together with a tongue and groove joint to form a seam-free surface. New systems do not require adhesive. Strip flooring can be laid on top of boards, concrete, or any level surface and can be bought in kits that include spacers (to ensure an even expansion gap) and a tamping block (for tapping joints together without damaging the grooves).

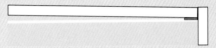

Cover the entire floor with underlay, joining the strips together with adhesive tape. If the subfloor is made of concrete, lay down a thick sheet of plastic to prevent moisture rising up through the underlay.

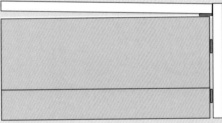

Place the grooved side of a strip along the longest wall. Put spacers in between to create an expansion gap. Insert the grooved side of a second strip into the first. Repeat until you are close to the wall. Cut the last strip to fit allowing for an expansion gap.

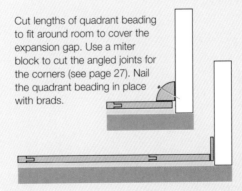

Cut lengths of quadrant beading to fit around room to cover the expansion gap. Use a miter block to cut the angled joints for the corners (see page 27). Nail the quadrant beading in place with brads.

laying carpeting

The easiest method is to fix carpet grippers—wooden or metal strips with metal spikes—around the edges of the room about ¼ inch from the baseboards, spikes facing toward the wall. Fix with short nails or, if the floor is solid, strong adhesive. Cut short strips to fit around alcoves and doorways. Cut the carpet padding to fit inside the strips.

Put the finished edge of the carpet along one wall making sure it butts right up to the edge. Push the carpet onto the spikes. Next, stretch the carpet across the room and fix it temporarily onto the gripper strip along the opposite wall. Work from the center toward the corners, pushing and stretching the carpet to fix it onto the spikes. Cut out triangles from the excess at the corners so the carpet can lay flat, then carefully cut along the edges using a utility knife. Use a long piece of wood or a metal straightedge to help push the carpet toward the wall and to act as a cutting edge. You will be exhausted and bad-tempered by now and vow to pay a professional in future, but hopefully, it will be perfectly okay and any imperfections will be hidden by furniture anyway.

things to know about windows and doors

Repairing, painting, and generally keeping doors and windows in good order not only makes your home look better but is also an opportunity to ensure that they are weatherproof and secure.

they set the style

Different architectural styles have different styles of windows and doors that have been designed to suit the character and proportion of the building. Beautiful windows enhance any home from the inside as well as out. If your windows are not architecturally significant, keeping them painted and in good repair will add to their appeal or detract from their bad points.

they spoil the effect

The wrong windows and doors can ruin an otherwise attractive building. Inappropriate window styles that show a lack of consideration for the history, proportion, materials, and construction of a property will not only be aesthetically displeasing but can be financially disadvantageous, often lowering the value of a home quite considerably.

they set the temperature

Open doors and windows let in warm summer sunshine and cooling breezes. Air circulation is necessary for a fresher, healthier environment for you and your building, but winter drafts will lower the temperature and increase the heating bills.

they keep things in

Including heat, the cat and your privacy. Well-fitting windows and doors will prevent valuable warmth from escaping and welcome sunshine in. Behind closed doors (and discreetly covered windows) you can create a complete world of your own, known only to you and your loved ones, where you can live a life suited to your own personality, passions, and predilections.

they keep things out

Including drafts, the weather, burglars, and other unwanted visitors. Solid doors and sturdy windows keep rain and wind in their place. Locked windows and doors will keep precious possessions safe and your insurance company happy.

repairing windows and doors

Doors and windows will be greatly enhanced if they open and shut properly.

doors

Squeaky doors may add atmosphere in a horror film but they are irritating on a daily basis. A squirt of oil on the hinges will solve the problem. Use the spray can variety and put the little tube over the nozzle so that you can aim it accurately into the hinge. If this doesn't work, or only works for a short while, it may be that the door is not hanging properly.

Whether you take on problems such as a sticking door, or one that doesn't shut, depends on the door, the frame, the hinges, and your physical strength. Solid wood doors are very heavy and not easy to handle on your own, so unless you have a strong friend to help you should probably call in an expert. Door frames are not always square, and distortions can be the result of age, heating, poor-quality wood, or just that they were badly hung in the first place.

In order to get a door to fit properly into a frame it is often necessary to remove wood from the edges and this involves using a plane—a tool with a sharp blade for shaving off thin strips of wood, so you will have to buy or borrow one. They are quite efficient and not too difficult to use (make sure the blade is sharp), but it is easy to get carried away and find you have shaved off too much.

If the door rattles and doesn't close properly, it could be that the latch bolt is not fitting into the strike plate hole. If it doesn't click into place when closed, it could be that the latch bolt is not reaching the strike plate hole in which case you should take off the plate and pack it out with some thin cardboard or wood filler, remembering you may need slightly longer screws when you put the plate back. Alternatively, the plate may be too near and the bolt doesn't have room to spring into the cavity, in which case remove the plate and chisel out a little more wood from the recess before screwing it back on.

It is not always necessary to take a door off in order to get it to fit better. Look at the hinges and check that the screws are all present and tight, that the hinge fits flush with the jamb, and that the hinges are positioned so that the door hangs at 90 degrees. Sometimes the screws work loose and tightening them, or replacing them with slightly longer ones, will pull the door back into position. If it still won't shut, find the place where it is not fitting into the jamb and either sand it down or plane off the excess (you may have to take the door off to do this). ALWAYS adjust the door, NOT the jamb.

door hinges

Hinges come in several forms. The simplest is the butt hinge with two flat rectangular flaps either side of the knuckle. One is screwed to the inside of the door jamb and the other to the edge of the door. They are set into a recess cut to the size and depth of the hinge flap so that they are flush with the woodwork. Just undo the screws on the frame if you need to remove the door. The rising butt hinge comes in two sections, one has a spindle and goes on the frame, the other has a socket which fits over the spindle. The door lifts when opened and so will rise above carpet then close on its own; the door can be lifted off without the need to undo screws (this can be difficult if they have been painted over). They come in left and right-handed opening versions.

Worn hinges cause doors to drop and therefore stick. Installing new hinges of the same size is easy, but use new, slightly larger screws to ensure they fit tightly into the old holes.

fitting a new door

Doors come in standard sizes and if these fit in your existing jamb you may wish to attempt hanging a new one, though it will involve some carpentry. However, if the standard size doesn't fit, or the door is very heavy, then leave it to an expert carpenter.

First, find a friend—you will need someone to help hold the door in position—and you will need two 4-inch butt hinges. Make sure the door fits into the jamb—there should be a gap of $1/16$ inch at the top and sides and minimum of $1/4$ inch at the bottom (more if you have thick carpeting). To check this, stand the door in position with wedges underneath that raise the door to the correct height above the floor. Make any necessary adjustments to the door edges using a plane.

With the door in the correct place, mark the position of the hinges 7 inches from the top and 10 inches from the bottom on both the door and the jamb.

Take the door down, stand it on its edge with the hinge side uppermost. Place the flap of the opened hinge against the marks, making sure that the knuckle projects beyond the edge (and the hinges are the right way up!). Draw around the flap with a pencil and mark the depth along on the edge.

Now comes the carpentry. With a chisel, make several cuts (the depth of the hinge) across the marked area, taking care not to cut across the pencil line, and also make cuts around the edge. You should then be able to pare away the wood to form a recess the exact dimensions of the hinge flap. Tidy up any rough bits with the chisel. Repeat for the other hinge.

Put the hinge flap in place, mark and drill pilot holes for the screws. Screw in place. Wedge the door in an open position with the unscrewed flaps against the marks on the door jamb. Making sure the knuckle is parallel to the frame, mark round the flap and repeat the carpentry.

Hang the door using one screw in each hinge and check that the door opens and closes smoothly. You may need to make the recesses a little deeper, or pack them out with thin cardboard. Put in the other screws.

hanging a door

If you have standard-sized doorways hanging a new door is not difficult and often easier than repairing an old one.

The simple butt hinge (left) is fine for most doors, but a rising butt hinge (right) lifts the door as it opens to fit over carpeting.

With the door in an open position place wedges underneath to hold it at the correct height, use the hinges to mark their position on the door jamb and the edge of the door.

Draw around hinge. Use a hammer and chisel to cut around the edge and make horizontal slots the same depth as the hinge across the marked area. Pare away the sections of wood.

Neaten up the finished cut out section, hold the hinge in place, and mark the position of the screws. Drill pilot holes and screw the hinge to the door.

fixing windows

Dealing with windows is not always an open and shut case.

windows

There are lots of types of windows, some wonderful and some not. They open in a variety of ways. Double-hung windows go up and down by means of a spring-mounted mechanism—or, if old, sash weights. Casement windows are hinged vertically to open like a door. Pivot windows have a hinge that allows them to rotate.

Most domestic window frames are made from wood but metal is not uncommon. Many new frames are made from coated aluminum while others combine wood and metal in quite complex units. Their construction is surprisingly complicated so don't even think about taking one out or putting in a new one. They are designed to be virtually maintenance-free; if they need a repair it is best to call in a window specialist.

Broken or cracked windows are dangerous and insecure as well as looking unkempt and unloved. Get a glazier to replace any glass. A professional will measure the replacement correctly, get it cut, take out the broken pieces, fit the new piece, fix it in place, and take all the broken glass away. Well worth the money. Glass is rather frightening and dangerous stuff to handle and with new metal window frames the glass is set into the frame and requires special fitting anyway.

Windows that open and close easily are a joy. If they don't, it is often an over-enthusiastic use of paint either inside or out that prevents them doing so. If the paint is relatively thin you can carefully cut along the join with a sharp-bladed knife and use a scraper to open up the gap. If the paint is thick and has seeped through all the joints you will have to resort to liquid paint stripper or a heat stripping gun.

If you can't shut the window properly, check where the window fits against the frame—especially the edge where the hinges are as drips of paint may be preventing a good seal. Hinges may also stiffen as a result of overpainting, a small amount of paint stripper may help get things moving. A squirt of oil will also loosen up clogged hinges.

Broken sash cords will not prevent you from opening a double-hung window but won't hold the window open. Replacing them involves taking the window out of the frame so get an expert to do it. Watch how it is done, then take on the next one.

Old window catches and handles are often coated with layers of paint which makes them stiff and less efficient. If the window frames are wood, putting on shiny new ones is relatively simple but the window hardware on old metal window frames is often part of the frame so you will need to rely on paint stripper to free them.

weatherproofing

Drafts have a knack of finding their way through even the tightest fitting doors and windows, but a wide variety of weatherproofing solutions are available to keep them in check. Some may not be suitable for metal door frames as they are not easy to screw into. The easiest and cheapest form of weatherstripping is a self-adhesive flexible foam strip with a peel-off backing which is stuck to the frame where it meets the door or window. It works well but will need replacing regularly.

A variety of weatherstripping materials are available for doors—wood, metal, rubber, plastic, or bristles attached to a strip (usually aluminum) that is screwed to the door frame. Threshold weatherstripping is screwed along the bottom of the door on the inside or outside depending on their construction and that of the door and frame. Among them are weather trims (screwed to the outside of the door and angled to shed water) and brush seals (a row of dense stiff bristles attached to a metal or wooden trim and screwed on the inside of the door). Other ingenious and sophisticated systems are best studied in the home improvement store where explanations of how they work and are fixed may be supplied by helpful assistants.

Weatherstripping for windows is much the same as for doors and varies according to the window type and construction. If any solution seems too expensive or will spoil the look of a window or door, you could consider keeping out slight drafts with heavy curtains.

An otherwise plain door can be transformed into a design feature with the addition of smart new door hardware. Designs have improved so much in the last few years that it is now possible to buy sleek, modern door handles at very realistic prices as well as countless styles to suit the character of your home.

Before buying, make sure you have the correct latch for your door. The mechanism is either fitted into a hole in the edge of the door, or is contained in a casing which is fitted onto the surface of the door with a latch keep screwed onto the outside edge of the door frame.

Fitting new knobs and handles on cabinets and dressers can give them a new lease of life. Simple pull handles are very easy as they are just screwed on—but make sure you position them correctly; crooked or uneven spacing will spoil the effect, so get out the tape measure and level.

things to know about walls and ceilings

The state of our walls and ceilings is important structurally as well as decoratively. You may wish to draw attention to them with bold colors and patterns or make them dissolve into the background with pale colorings or remove them altogether. Either way they cannot be ignored and will benefit from care and attention.

what they are made of

Solid walls are made of stone, brick, concrete block, or solid concrete. Outside walls are usually thicker than internal ones. Inside, walls are usually covered with plaster.

Uneven surfaces such as stone walls in old houses have a coarser rendered finish. Such homes may have inside walls made from laths—narrow strips of wood nailed to a framework and covered with lime-based plaster—which, depending on the condition of the building, is hard and strong or weak and crumbly.

A cavity wall is a double external wall with a gap in between, which may be filled with insulation material.

Wallboard and plywood can be fixed to solid walls for a smooth surface. A stud partition wall consists of a wooden framework with sheet material, usually drywall, nailed to it. Drywall is often skimmed with a thin layer of plaster to give a smooth finish and cover up any joints.

they are never "true"

As discussed in measuring, walls and ceilings are rarely perfectly straight or their surfaces completely smooth. For this reason, they don't always join neatly to baseboards, door, and window frames, or each other. Very uneven, undulating surfaces are part of the "character" of an old home, but in newer buildings it could be a sign of something wrong so get it looked at.

what they do

Load-bearing walls have an important role supporting and strengthening a building. If you want to remove such a wall, you need to replace it with something, usually a steel I-beam, which must be specified by a qualified engineer. Definitely one for an expert!

Partition walls only divide up space so it is possible to take them away without the building falling down. Only an expert will know which are non-supporting walls, so DON'T do it yourself!

they can be thin

The sound-proofing efficiency of walls depends on their construction. Party walls which divide one building from another are often built of brick, stone, or concrete and are dense enough to provide adequate insulation against the noise from normal daily lives. Internal partition walls, which are often a cavity construction, are not as effective at keeping sound in or out. Apartments in converted houses don't always have properly constructed party walls and floors, which can cause a problem. Foam, styrene, or purpose-made insulation boarding can be incorporated into the wall construction.

Minimalism may look chic but hard surfaces reflect sound, creating an echoey and unfriendly ambience. Wooden paneling and wallcoverings provide a gentler, warmer environment. Carpets, curtains, soft furniture, and books also absorb noise.

fixing walls and ceilings

Cracks on wall and ceiling surfaces are common. They can be caused for a variety of the reasons from very minor to rather worrying. Fine cracks in plaster are often the result of shrinkage due to drying, heat, etc., or vibration from impact such as knocking in nails or drilling a hole.

Bigger cracks appear through settlement due to minor building work in adjacent rooms or buildings, or the effects of unusually extreme temperatures. Large cracks or cracks that keep getting bigger can indicate structural faults, so get an expert to have a look.

surface tension

Holes in walls can be dealt with quite easily but holes in ceilings are trickier. Working on walls is easier as they are vertical and you have gravity on your side. Ceilings are, and give you, a pain in the neck. One false move and it could end up on the floor. Large holes in ceilings are a job for the experts.

Small to medium-size cracks, holes, and dents can be filled with an all-purpose patching compound. This comes as a powder to which you add water but a ready-mixed version in an air-tight plastic bucket (which is exactly the right consistency and very convenient, but much more expensive) is also available. Apply using a putty knife or wallboard knife. The mixture shrinks slightly when it dries so leave the compound slightly raised from the surface.

When the repair is set, use sand paper to smooth out the bumps. If there is a lot to remove use a coarse paper first and finish with fine. Wrapping the san paper around a sanding block will give a more even finish.

holed up

Old screw holes are deep, so poke damp newspaper into the hole before applying the patching compound. For bigger, deeper holes use a lightweight coarse plaster mix which, when mixed with water, forms a nice thick, easy to handle mixture. When it is dry, sand it down with a coarse-grit sand paper before applying a top layer of smooth compound.

Repairing really big holes usually involves replastering. This is a skill acquired through years of practice and if you value your home, and your sanity, you will call in an expert plasterer.

filled in

Getting patching compound into the gaps around frames, baseboards, and the joints between walls and ceilings, can be difficult and messy, so use an acrylic caulk. It comes in a tube with a pointed nozzle that fits into a caulking gun allowing you to shoot accurately into crevices.

fun and fancy

Decorative cornices, moldings, and ceiling rosettes are often damaged or have lost their definition through layers of paint. If your home is an architectural gem, leave any repairs to the expert as the value of your home could be seriously affected by poor and insensitive workmanship. However, in the Victorian and Edwardian era even quite modest homes had moldings that were mass-produced.

If you have the patience you can restore cornices to their former glory by picking out all the old paint. Fortunately, ceilings are usually painted with water-based paint that can be removed by soaking. Wet a small area using a plant spray or sponge to see how easily it will come off. Use various sizes of

screwdrivers and a soft brush to remove
the clogged paint. Bear in mind that the
process will involve a lot of water and
mess. If oil-based paint has been used,
it will have to be removed with paint
stripper—a very unpleasant task.

If you can't face this lengthy task,
opt for a good wash using a brush, or
just brush out all the dust and dirt before
painting over it. Providing you don't draw
attention to it with contrasting colors, it
will look fine.

safe as houses

It is wise to be security conscious but there is no need to be paranoid. Some home insurance companies insist on a certain level of security before providing cover. Find out before embarking on any security improvements as certain locks and bolts may be specified.

While it is nice to feel no one can get in, remember once inside with all bolts and locks secured you will not be able to get out easily. Having to fiddle with keys in a fire could be fatal, and if you are ill valuable time could be wasted getting to you. Make sure keys are kept in an accessible place (but not handy for burglars), leave a spare set with someone reliable (not often out or away), and give details to close friends and family.

door locks, bolts, and spyholes

The two types of deadbolt locks most frequently used are the cylinder rim and the mortise. The cylinder rim lock is used mainly on front doors. A small knob or handle on the inside turns a spring lock to open the door. When the door closes it automatically springs back into place and can only be opened from the outside using a key. An extra turn with the key from the outside will lock it into position so that it cannot be opened from the inside.

The mechanism of a mortise lock is fitted into a hole in the edge of the door jamb and must be locked and unlocked with a key, although some can be opened from the inside with a knob or handle.

Installing cylinder rim locks is not too difficult but they are quite sophisticated mechanisms so it is usual to ask a locksmith. He will make sure everything lines up, works properly and conforms to requirements for insurance.

Fitting a mortise lock involves cutting a deep slot in the edge of the door—drill a row of holes to the required depth and then gouge out the rest with a chisel—in which to fit the "lock body" and then a shallower slot in the door jamb for the bolt or latch. Now drill a hole into the door to give access to the keyhole—a locksmith will do this accurately.

Replacing a lock is easy if you get one of similar size and make to fit into the existing holes. Take the old lock to a locksmith or home improvement store to make sure. If your keys have been lost or stolen you only need to replace the internal mechanism—a locksmith will supply a new one complete with new keys.

Hinge bolts screw into the edge of the door—near the hinges for strength—and fit into a recess in the door frame when the door is closed. Drill a shallow hole in the door for screwing the bolt into, and another in the frame opposite. Chisel out a recess for the locking plate.

Bolts add extra security but as they can only be operated from inside you will be locking yourself in. Make sure you can open them quickly in case of emergency.

Rack bolts fit into the edge of the door and are operated by a key. You will have to drill three holes, one for the barrel, one for the key and one in the frame for the bolt to fit into. Be careful to drill straight into the door and the frame—veering off at angle could damage the door and the bolt won't fit properly. Mark the position of the keyhole using a try square.

Spyholes are useful for checking out a visitor before choosing whether or not to open the door. They are simple to install and can be adjusted to fit any thickness of door. Drill a hole right through the center of the door at eye level. Insert the barrel of the viewer from the outside and screw in the eyepiece from the inside.

A security chain is another wise precaution. The fixed end of the chain is screwed to the door frame and the loose end fits into a fixing plate screwed to the door. For convenience, position it just below the lock.

window locks

Window locks are a good idea and often required for insurance purposes. There are a number of different styles to suit different window styles. They work on the principle of locking the window to the frame (or for double-hung windows, locking the windows together) either with a screw or bolt. They are usually operated with a key. Some can be locked manually but must be opened with a key. Many use a standard key which is widely available (and therefore can be bought by burglars) but others have keys cut in several hundred variations.

Newer windows are supplied with integral locks and lockable stays, but to secure more traditional, wooden windows it is easy to screw on locks; others will need holes drilling for the bolts and the key. Patio doors are especially inviting to intruders, so make sure they are fitted with the correct type of lock and fit them top and bottom to prevent the doors from being lifted out of the frame.

security lights and alarms

An outside light operated from inside illuminates visitors and indicates the house is occupied. A security light that comes on when approached will illuminate dark doorways, deter intruders, and enable you to find the keyhole in the dark. Though relatively inexpensive and easy to install, outdoor lighting involves drilling through outside walls and taking electricity outside where it needs special insulation to cope with wet weather. This is, therefore, a job for the expert.

Alarm and surveillance systems should always be installed by a reputable company, as the systems are sophisticated and complicated to set up. Installation will affect your home insurance policy which may impose stringent regulations. There are several do-it-yourself versions on the market but you will need expert advice on how to set it up and approval from your insurance company, so, once again, leave it to the experts.

Connecting a light or a radio to an automatic time-switch will give the impression that your home is occupied. They can be set to switch on and off several times during the day. However, the regularity of the timing may tip off a

watchful burglar so use it for short periods of absence, or alternatively invest in a more sophisticated switch that will change the timings throughout the week or can be set to random switching.

smoke alarms

Fire can be devastating to property and life so every home needs a smoke detector that gives off a piercing wail when in contact with smoke. There are two main types. Photoelectric devices detect large quantities of smoke produced by slow-burning fires. Ionization devices are more sensitive to small particles of smoke as produced by hot blazing fires. Fortunately, detectors are available that combine both systems and as the incidence of both types of fire can never be discounted it would be wise to opt for one of these.

Battery operated detectors are easy to put up. Don't put them in kitchens or bathrooms where steam can set them off, and don't place them near sources of heat. Hallways and landings are good places. Put one on each floor and if you live in an apartment find a position that is near the bedroom. Replace batteries every year and check the alarm every month to ensure it is working.

beauty treatments

home makeovers with paints, papers, and tiles

Now that fashion relates to interiors as well as clothes, and the wrong floor covering can be just as much a faux pas as the wrong skirt length, knowing how to keep your decor up to date will allow you to entertain friends without fear of losing your fashion cred. You may not be able to afford architectural schemes and designer furniture, but whether you favor minimalism or country chic, it is possible to create a sense of a style with paint and wallpaper and a little pruning and preening of your possessions.

Keeping it simple is wisest and easiest. Fortunately the simple, uncluttered look is currently very chic, but it also provides a good basis for a more decorative approach. Clearing out a room ready for decorating is an opportunity for a big clear-out of unwanted stuff and outdated clutter ready for a fresh look and perhaps a fresh start. Favorite belongings will come into their own when placed in a newly decorated environment and it will be easier to throw away those that don't show up so well.

Preparation is important if you want to achieve a good finish. Filling in holes, washing and sanding down old paintwork can be tedious (and not as much fun as the actual painting or papering), but it is satisfying and produces a more professional-looking result. Paint is easy to use, especially latex which can be put on quickly with a roller or large brush. Eco-friendly, water-based gloss and eggshell finishes are now available which are much

easier to use, are less smelly than the oil-based versions and, as an added bonus, the brushes can be washed out in water. Wallpapering may not be quite so easy as slapping on paint, but it isn't difficult if you stick to one wall or uncomplicated spaces. It is useful for covering up a particularly bad surface, and wallpaper is making a comeback—look out for new designs by trendy designers and revamped fifties retro styles.

It is quite possible to change the whole character of your home with a single can of paint so be adventurous—you can always paint over it if you hate it. Try out some of the fabulous colors on those tempting paint charts and impress trend-conscious visitors by regularly repainting a wall in the latest fashionable hue. A coat of paint not only freshens an interior but can be used to unify and create an illusion of space. Several small rooms will feel part of a single space if they are painted the same color, and a collection of different style chairs will look like a set if given the same treatment. Bold colors add drama and focus while patterned wallpaper can bring a touch of retro or romance.

Even the most uninspiring environment can be improved by a little tender loving care. A lick of paint can bring light into a dark room or a feeling of intimacy in a large space. It can also turn a perfectly ordinary home into a wild wonderland so don't be timid; try it!

essential paint equipment

Painting methods vary depending on the type of paint used and the finish required.

paintbrushes

Paintbrushes come in all sorts of shapes, sizes, types of bristle, and prices. The least expensive brushes—often sold in bargain sets—will shed their bristles and won't hold the paint well so are best avoided. The most expensive have high-quality, densely packed bristles for ease of application and a smooth finish, but unless you are planning a lot of decorating (and are prepared to take great care of your brushes) go for a medium price range. Check that the bristles spring back when you bend them. Real bristle is very good as each hair tapers naturally to a point, but there are some excellent good-quality synthetic bristles.

If you intend to use a brush for painting your walls, invest in a good-quality flat, 6-inch wide latex paintbrush. A range of narrow brushes will be needed for window and door casings and trim moldings and a slightly wider brush for larger areas of woodwork, such as doors. Narrow cutting-in brushes have the bristles cut at an angle to make it easier to get right to the edge when painting muntins.

paint rollers

Rollers are fantastic for covering large areas of wall or ceiling quickly and evenly. They consist of a roller cover or "sleeve" which fits onto a metal rod or wire cage attached to a handle. Most covers are either sheepskin (real or synthetic) or foam. Long-pile sheepskin holds a lot of paint but medium-pile is more manageable. Foam covers are less efficient as they tend to leave air bubbles on the surface.

Rollers are used with a metal or plastic pan, which has a ribbed area that slopes down to a paint reservoir. Roller and pan sets are often very inexpensive and although the quality may not always be tip-top, you can just throw them away after use. If, however, you are more ecologically minded, buy a good-quality set and wash thoroughly after use—replacement roller covers are available.

Long-handled roller extensions are available for painting ceilings and floors, which makes the job easier. Other sizes and shapes can be found including a small roller on a long handle for painting behind radiators, shaped rollers for painting into corners, and small dense foam rollers for use with gloss or eggshell paint for large flat areas such as doors and bath panels.

paint pads

Paint pads are very useful for painting large flat areas and are generally thought to be as good as a roller. Square or rectangular in shape, they consist of a layer of short mohair pile attached to a foam layer, which gives flexibility and keeps the pad in contact with uneven surfaces. The pad is fixed to a plastic frame with an integrated handle. Also sold in sets with a pan, the best type of pan has a loading roller to ensure the paint is distributed evenly on the pad.

paint buckets

Paint buckets are plastic or metal. You can decant a smaller, more manageable amount of paint into them when you are using a brush. Especially useful if you are on a ladder.

drop cloths

Painting is a messy business so make sure you have enough drop cloths to protect furniture, floors, and other surfaces from paint splashes and the water and debris from washing and stripping down walls. Old sheets and bedspreads are ideal, but use plastic sheeting underneath on vulnerable surfaces as big blobs of paint will soak through fabric.

masking tape

Masking tape is perfect for keeping paint off glass when painting window trims and paint off carpeting when painting baseboards. Use to get a straight edge for different colored panels and borders.

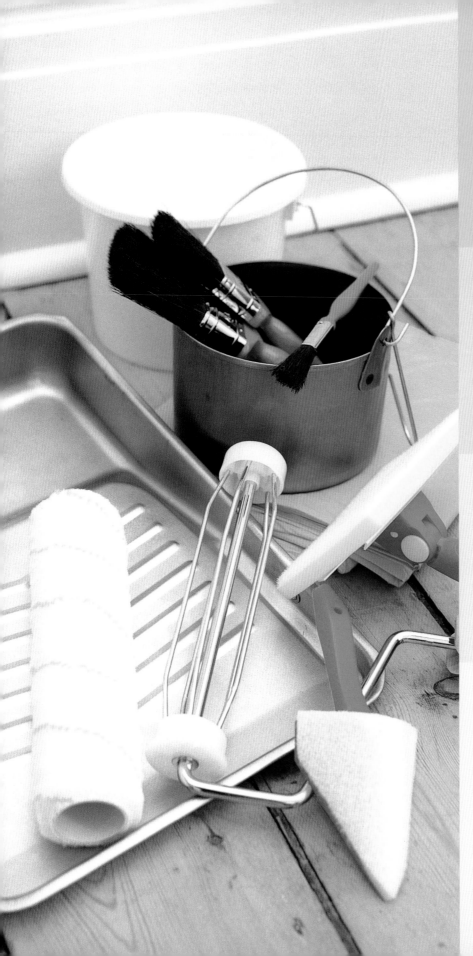

preparation

The right tools makes preparation easier and more effective.

straightedge scrapers
Used for removing wallpaper or paint, they have flat, nonflexible blades.

shaped paintscrapers
Useful for removing paint from awkward corners and moldings.

wallpaper perforation tools
Used to puncture the surface of coated or painted wallpaper.

steam strippers
A steam plate, held against the wall to penetrate the paper. Can be rented.

heat gun
Heat and soften oil-based paint so that it can be scraped off easily.

liquid paint strippers
Will soften paint so it can be scraped away.

scrubbing brushes
Useful for cleaning dirt from corners.

wire brushes
Will remove flakes of paint or rust but can be a bit harsh so use with care.

dry paintbrushes
Can be used as dusting brushes to clean corners and keyholes.

preparing paintwork

When decorating, the end result will look better and last longer if you do a proper job of preparing the old before adding the new. The thought of stripping the walls and sanding down paintwork may fill you with dread, but it can become a cleansing experience for your mind as well as your home. Take out unwanted fixtures, but keep things that would be expensive or difficult to replace. If walls are papered, strip them back to bare plaster to provide a good surface for painting or papering and to reveal any cracks or damp problems.

preparing walls and ceilings

Stripping wallpaper can be hard work, but there are ways to make it easier. Choose a discreet corner and remove a small piece of wallpaper to see how many layers there are, what type of paper it is, whether it will come away easily, and the state of the wall underneath. If large amounts of plaster come away with the paper, it may be best to leave well enough alone and paint over the paper. Alternatively, get a builder in to replaster.

Uncoated paper should come off easily with soap and hot water. Apply generously with a sponge until the paper can be scraped off. Repeat as many times as necessary. Steaming is also a very efficient way to remove wallpaper. Coated wallpapers, or paper that has been painted over, will need scoring with a perforation tool or the edge of a scraper to allow the steam or water to soak through. If the paper is vinyl coated you can usually remove it by simply lifting the corners of the vinyl and pulling it away from its backing paper, which can then be removed with water or steam.

Once you have stripped the old wallpaper, remove any debris and dirt with a scraper or wallboard knife, then wash down the walls thoroughly before painting or repapering. Use warm soapy water and finish with a sponge or cloth rinsed frequently in clean water. If the old paint surface is rough with loose flakes of paint use a wet-and-dry sand paper (dry sanding produces too much dust) to smooth the edges. Alternatively, flat nylon scourers will scrub off any loose bits of paint and smooth down the surface.

If, after filling in the holes and cracks (as described in the previous chapter), the surface still looks a bit flaky you can give the wall a coat of general-purpose sealer to seal the surface—just follow the instructions on the can. Paint and wallpaper adhesive will not adhere to old distemper, so brush away any loose material and apply a stabilizing primer.

If the underlying paint is gloss or eggshell, it will be necessary to wash down the wall with a TSP solution, rinse, and then sand with a medium wet-and-dry sand paper. To seal new or newly revealed bare plaster, dilute the first coat of paint (half paint, half water) or seal as above. Put one coat of paint on the wall before filling all the holes, as some may not show once they have been painted over.

If, despite priming, sanding, and using filling techniques, the wall surface is still uneven, you can either learn to love the "distressed" effect or apply extra coats of paint with a roller to form a slightly textured finish that will soften the blemishes. Alternatively, cover the entire wall with a plain wall-lining paper (use a thick, textured variety for very uneven surfaces) that can be painted.

Cover stains such as damp or mildew with a stain block or recommended primer, but address the source of the stain first to prevent the stains reappearing. Also, covering damp with an impervious coating will only send the moisture elsewhere where it could do more damage.

preparing woodwork

Prepare old woodwork for repainting by washing and rinsing the surface, using a TSP solution or detergent. A flat nylon scourer is good for getting rid of blemishes and will also help break down the surface. Pay particular attention to baseboards, which are often scuffed, the areas around door handles and window catches, which will be greasy, and make sure you get into all corners, especially on window trims. Sand down any old drips and wrinkles. Hard gloss paint may need further sanding down with fine wet-and-dry sand paper. Repair chips and damaged areas with primer, building up the surface with several coats if necessary, sanding between each. Wipe with a clean cloth dipped in mineral spirits to get rid of any remaining dust and grease.

If possible, paint over the existing paint, as stripping it off is a messy, time-consuming business. However, if the old paint surface is really bad, or the buildup of paint is the cause of ill-fitting windows and doors, stripping might be necessary.

A heat gun softens paint so it can be scraped off easily, often several coats in one go. The nozzle is held about 2 inches from the surface and moved slowly back and forth until the paint blisters. Remove the paint with a paint scraper. Different shaped nozzles can be used to focus the heat or diffuse it and, on narrow muntins, will keep heat away from the glass.

If you think this sounds scary, the alternative is to use a chemical paint stripper, which is no picnic either. Follow the instructions carefully, allow plenty of ventilation, wear a mask to protect against the fumes, and wear good protective gloves as the stripper will burn your skin on contact. Strippers usually consist of a thick viscous liquid that is dabbed onto the paint until it blisters. How easy this is depends on how many layers of paint there are. It is better to keep applying more stripper until it has penetrated all the layers and the paint (or most of it) can be scraped off all at once. Liquid paint strippers are not suitable for use on large areas as the fumes are too overpowering. If you are stripping paint ready for repainting, some residue will not be a problem as long as it is sanded and free of grease. But if you want to strip down to the bare wood, you will have to work very hard to get every bit off, using a chemical paint stripper or a combination of this and a heat gun.

lead paint

Until the 1960s, lead was widely used in oil-based paints and primers. Removing these paints can be hazardous as dust containing lead particles can be inhaled and absorbed through the skin. You are advised to obtain a leaflet about this before redoing old woodwork. If possible, leave existing lead paint in place, smooth any surface defects with wet-and-dry sand paper or steel wool dampened with mineral spirits, and simply paint over it. If it is necessary to remove old paint, avoid dust by using a chemical paint stripper rather than a dry abrasive or use a heat gun set at a low temperature to avoid the release of toxic fumes. Wear protective clothing and a face mask. Any exposed skin should be washed thoroughly afterward and the room should also be washed down with water and detergent. All peelings should be collected and placed in a sealed bag. A domestic vacuum cleaner is not powerful enough to remove all lead traces in dust and paint flakes, so rent an industrial-standard vacuum cleaner.

primers and sealers

Some surfaces may need special treatment in order to make them suitable for painting.

stabilizing primer
A white or clear liquid used on walls to bind dusty, powdery, and flaky surfaces.

wood primer
Available in oil-based, water-based, acrylic, or aluminum forms. Used on new or bare wood to seal and prevent subsequent applications of paint soaking into the wood.

general-purpose primer
Used for wood, metal, and plaster as well as porous building materials. Look out for water-based versions.

metal primer
Prevents corrosion and provides a key for paint. Rust inhibitors also available.

general-purpose sealer
A clear sealer that can be used to prime or size surfaces.

stain sealer
Prevents stains bleeding through paint.

undercoat paint
A flat paint used on woodwork to cover primer and minor imperfections. Provides a smooth, dense surface for topcoats. Particularly effective if the topcoat is a dark color or high gloss finish.

essential points about paint

For a fraction of the price of a Prada handbag you can completely transform your room, and perhaps even your life. If you like to change your interior style as frequently as your clothes, then a coat of paint will do it.

it's colorful
Paint comes in the proverbial "bewildering" variety of colors, but there are lots of specialist and designer paint ranges that can help you make up your mind by selecting and combining all the latest, must-have colors.

it's confusing
It always used to be gloss or eggshell paint for woodwork and latex for walls, but now you can buy paint in all sorts of finishes as well as colors—from glamorous satin and glitter paints to posh flat-oil finishes and distemper.

it's easy
Water-based paints are easy to use. It is not too difficult to produce a nice even finish, especially if you use a roller. Some paints guarantee to cover in one coat and come ready-to-use in a pan with a roller or pad, so you just have to peel the lid off and paint away.

it's messy
Paint rollers may be efficient at covering walls, but they will also cover your hair, face, glasses, and unsuspecting pets. Overfilled brushes cover your hands and arms while oil-based paints are thicker, stickier, and hard to remove from unwanted areas.

it's worth it
Paint can change the look and mood of a room, making it look cleaner, bigger, cozier, sexier, smarter, or just nicer. It is a well-known fact that when selling a home, a coat of paint can turn it from an ordinary dwelling into a desireable residence.

it's tricky
Painting woodwork is more difficult than walls; smaller areas take longer to paint as you must use a smaller brush. New wood will need a coat of primer first and then, ideally, an undercoat. Gloss, eggshell, satin, and flat finishes need careful application to avoid drips.

it's quick
Using latex paint and a roller it is possible to cover a huge area of wall in a very short time. Even with a brush it doesn't take too long. Modern paints dry quickly so you can put on the next coat in as little as two hours and finish a whole room in a morning.

it's slow
Oil-based paints not only take longer to apply, they also take longer to dry. You may have to wait up to 24 hours before putting on the next coat. For a perfect finish, you may also have to sand the surface between coats, which can take ages.

types of paint

Buying paint used to be simple: you used water-based latex for walls and oil-based gloss or satin paint for woodwork. Nowadays we are presented with not only a vast range of colors, but also a confusing selection of types and finishes from the cheerfully cheap to the ultra chic. They do, however, divide fairly logically into paints for walls and paints for woodwork.

Walls are mostly painted with latex which is water-based, while woodwork, which needs a harder, more durable surface, has traditionally been painted with oil-based paints. However, the demand for paints that are easy to apply, dry quickly, and are eco-friendly has led to the development of many more water-based paints and primers that are suitable for use on wood and metal.

It is important to read what it says on the paint container. All information on contents, safety precautions, preparation, application, drying times, coverage, and how to clean brushes is printed on the container together with any special features.

paint for walls

Paint provides a pick-me-up for tired walls which can be transformed in an afternoon.

latex paint

A water-based latex is best for walls. It is easy to apply and to wash out of brushes, rollers, and your hair. It is available in a flat or satin finish. One-coat latex paints are available in a limited range of colors and often come in a pan ready for rollering. They often have additives such as vinyl to give a smoother, more stable, durable, and washable surface. Latex can be applied with a brush, roller, or pad. As well as being easy to use, latex is readily available in a huge range of colors. What's more, it is quick drying—further coats can be applied in 2–4 hours—and has minimal odor.

distemper

Distemper consists of pigments and binders (glues and natural resins) dispersed in water and must be used correctly in order to achieve an even finish. Usually produced by specialist companies, distemper varies in type and composition, so always follow all instructions on the can. It can be applied on top of existing latex, but bare plaster will require several thin coats. Its dense, chalky finish is historically correct and particularly suited to old properties. It is especially good for moldings which become clogged and lose definition if painted with standard latex paints. However, distemper is less stable than latex and will rub off, so it is unsuitable for areas of high wear such as staircases. Apply with a brush or, on delicate or fragile plasterwork, a spray. It looks wonderful, but if you are after a quick fix this isn't the paint for you.

other paints

There are several "special effect" paints on the market, but the effect is not always successful and they do require certain application skills. Simple is best, and smart handywomen will keep it plain.

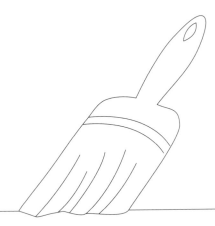

paint for woodwork

Freshly painted woodwork provides the finishing touch to a room.

gloss paint

Gloss paint has a hard-wearing finish with a reflective surface quality. It shows up all imperfections and needs careful application to avoid sags and drips. For best results, use over an undercoat paint. Traditionally gloss paint is oil-based and therefore smelly and slow to dry, but water-based versions are now available. One-coat gloss paint saves time but can look a bit thin. Nondrip gloss paint is cleaner but can be a bit glutinous and difficult to apply. If used with an undercoat paint a single topcoat of gloss paint is usually sufficient. Oil-based gloss requires up to 16 hours' drying time and will not fully harden for several days.

other paints

Oil-based paints with semi-gloss, eggshell, and satin finishes, all have a slightly reflective surface quality. Much easier to use than gloss paint, they won't show up every imperfection. Use with an undercoat paint to get a denser color.

Water-based versions of these paints are now widely available.

Flat paint has a dead mat finish. It can also be used on plaster and papered walls. The versions produced by specialist companies are usually oil-based.

how much paint?

The amount of paint required for a job will depend on the type and make of paint, the color, the state and porosity of the existing surface, and the method of application. Commercially produced latex paints are generally quite thick and will cover well, though some brands, and inexpensive paints, are thinner. Some specialist paints will need extra coats, as their ingredients tend to have fewer additives that aid coverage. Details of estimated coverage will be printed on the container. The average coverage of one gallon of latex paint is between 500-540 square feet but, as discussed above, this will vary. Extra coats will be necessary if you are covering a dark color or pattern. Pure, deep colors, such as bright yellows or reds, will need extra coats to achieve an even depth of color

and this will usually be indicated on the paint container.

Rollers are fast and will cover in fewer, thicker coats. The brush method is slower but tends to use less paint than rollering as it is a little more controlled. Make sure you buy enough paint to do the whole room. Different batches of paint will differ slightly and if you are using a color-mixing service bear in mind that the amounts of color dispensed can vary slightly each time the color is mixed, and that machines in different stores will rarely produce an exact match.

applying paint

How you decide to apply your paint will depend not only on the paint but also on your personality. If you want fast results you will love using a roller, but if you are a bit of a perfectionist and enjoy art then the pleasure of the brush may appeal. Whichever method you choose, remember to unscrew all light switches, fixtures, and outlets so that you can paint behind them for a neater appearance.

using a paint roller

Before painting walls and ceilings you'll have to do some "cutting in" which involves using a small brush to paint around all the edges—ceiling/wall joints, corners, baseboards, light switches, and light fixtures—as well as the narrow areas where a roller won't fit. Pour paint into the deep end of the roller pan so that it comes up to the level of the end of the slope. Choose a roller no more than 9 inches wide (anything bigger becomes too tiring to use). Load the roller by dipping it into the paint and then rolling it up and down on the ribbed section to distribute the paint evenly (with a clean, dry roller you may have to do this several times). Place the roller on the surface, using enough pressure to prevent it spinning around on its own, and transfer the paint to the wall. Keep the roller in contact with the surface at all times, distributing the paint evenly in all directions, but don't try to cover too large an area with one load as the coverage will be too thin and may lead to an uneven,

patchy finish. Try not to overload the paint roller as this will increase the drip-spray count. Use a long handle attachment for painting ceilings—but wear a hat!

Small rollers are great for applying eggshell or gloss paint onto large areas such as doors, but keep to one direction for your finishing strokes.

using a paint pad

Using a paint pad is much the same as using a roller, but the paint is loaded evenly by passing it over the roller in the paint pan. Keep the pad flat against the surface and paint in all directions using a gentle sweeping action.

using a paintbrush

Applying thick paint with a brush is hard work and it is sometimes easier to thin the paint slightly and apply extra coats. It is important not to overload the brush as this leads to messy painting (and paint running down your arms), so dip only a third of the bristle area into the paint and tap off any excess on the side of the can before painting. How you hold the brush will depend on personal preference and comfort as well as the size of the brush and the type of paint. Holding it like a pen will give more control and makes sense for narrow brushes on woodwork, but for wide brushes (especially on ceilings) it may feel more comfortable to hold the handle firmly in your fist. The most important thing is to transfer the paint onto the surface in vertical strokes—not dabs—

and spread it out using horizontal strokes as well. On large areas don't brush out too thinly at the edges as you will get an uneven finish. Work from right to left if you are right-handed (the other way around if you are left-handed) so that your arm is away from your body.

For woodwork, especially oil-based paints and gloss finishes, the brushstrokes should follow the grain of the wood and be vertical or horizontal (according to the direction of the frame or baseboard) to prevent brushmarks spoiling the finished surface.

To get a neat line along baseboards, around door and window frames, and between ceilings and wall, place the brush a short distance away from the edge and press down so that the bristles fan out to reach the edge. If you can't do this without losing control of the brush, paint, or your temper, then use masking tape. It is, however, always a good idea to use masking tape around the edges of the glass when painting windows. A variety of simple plastic shields are available to keep paint off floors and glass, but as they need to be held in position they can get in the way and prevent you from using your spare hand for something more useful, like holding paint.

Brushes can shed a few bristles when they are new, so before using them on woodwork (where shedding bristles will be a great nuisance and spoil the finish) break them in by using with latex first.

perfect paintwork

As long as you prepare surfaces well and take reasonable care when applying paint, the finished result should look fine. Small defects and slightly imperfect finishes rarely stand out once the furniture is in place. Woodwork needs more attention than walls. For a very beautiful, high-quality finish on woodwork apply two or three topcoats, sanding with steel wool or wet-and-dry sand paper between each coat. Follow instructions on the paint container and allow the paint to fully harden before recoating.

avoiding common problems

drips, runs, and sags Make sure there is not too much paint on your brush/roller and brush it out across the surface.

brushmarks Use a good-quality brush and make sure it is perfectly clean. Brush out runs as you go along but don't attempt to brush them out once the surface has started to dry.

specks and lumps on the surface Make sure your brush is clean and that the surface is completely free from dirt and dust, including in the corners. During a break put the lids back on paint cans and put brushes, rollers, or pads (complete with their pans) inside a plastic bag, tied or folded, to stop them drying out and attracting dust and dirt.

flaking Ensure that you have prepared the surface properly by getting rid of all loose material and grease spots. Once you have washed the walls make sure they are dry before you begin to paint.

poor finish Remember to sand the surface before painting and allow sufficient drying time between coats. Do not apply your paint too thinly and be sure to apply enough coats.

patchy finish Paint in mainly vertical strokes to get good coverage and only take a break when an entire wall is complete. For a good gloss finish on doors, apply the last strokes vertically.

cleaning up

The worst thing about decorating is cleaning up afterward. If you have been a diligent painter, it should just be a matter of folding the drop cloths (taking care not to shake dust onto still-wet paint) and standing back to admire your work. However, there are usually a few stray splashes that should be cleaned off immediately with a damp cloth (or a cloth soaked in mineral spirits if the paint is oil-based) while bigger blobs can be removed with a scraper. Be careful not to disturb soft paint and don't try to neaten edges until the paint is hard.

Try to wash brushes and other equipment as soon as you have finished as the paint will harden and be more difficult to remove. If this isn't possible, put them in a plastic bag or leave them to soak in plenty of water. If you have been using water-based paints, wash brushes, rollers, and pads in plenty of warm soapy water and rinse until the water is clear. Flex the bristles of brushes to make sure no paint remains in the roots. Squeeze or shake out surplus moisture and leave to dry naturally. For oil-based paints, wipe off excess paint on newspaper, then flex the bristles in a jar of mineral spirits (or special solvent as indicated on the can) to dissolve the remaining paint. Wash with hot soapy water and rinse. Repeat if necessary until the brush is clean. Keep paintbrushes in shape by folding paper around the bristles and securing with a rubber band.

paint projects

With the availability of a huge range of paints and palettes to suit all personalities, it is up to you to decide whether to be restrained or go for drama and adventure. Inspiration can come from a variety of sources—a postcard, a trip to a museum or gallery, a bunch of flowers, or just the desire to add a little more color to your life.

white space

If you long for large white, light-filled spaces but your own home is somewhat confined, clear out your clutter and paint your walls, ceiling, floor, woodwork, and even furniture in fresh, clean, dazzling white.

dash of drama

Use shiny gloss paint for drama, glamor, and hard-edged modernism. Paint a whole room in a bright color but keep furnishings to a minimum. Alternatively, paint just one wall or a single panel—use masking tape for a perfect edge, and leave a gap around the edges for more impact and neater joints. Use a contrasting color for window and door trim, and why not paint each door in a different, bright color.

cool shades

Use combinations of hints, tints, and tones of a single color to add variety without contrast. Choose a collection of the new whites—from pale creams to greeny grays—for an amazingly subtle look. Or go for twiggy, pebbly colors to create an aura of natural harmony. Use lots of different colors but keep control by choosing similar moods or shades of each.

touch of history

The vogue for historical correctness has led to the development of new types of paint based on old "recipes." The colors are wonderfully flat and dense. They bring old properties back to life and give new places a sense of identity. The range of colors is limited, but they share a similar quality which means they all work well together. Dark colored woodwork looks contemporary as well as authentic.

essential points about wallcoverings

For the last few years, paint has been the favored finish for walls, especially with people who are more adventurous with color. Wallpaper, however, is making a comeback. Blousy roses and spriggy flowers have never lost their appeal, but the revival of interest in fifties and sixties design has brought bold geometrics back into the limelight. Even if you are a firm fan of plain walls, you may need to paper in order to provide a good surface on which to paint.

it's a cover-up

Obliterate cracked, lumpy, bumpy plaster with a covering of good thick paper which can be painted or exist in its own right. Bring a room back to life with a fresh layer of wallpaper on top of old, dirty, dated, and impossible-to-remove paper. Lose imperfect edges, ugly features, and funny angles in a riot of pattern.

it's tricky

Those endless comedy sketches can be played out for real in your own home as you wrestle with sticky paper that appears to have a mind of its own. Matching patterns, cutting around light fixtures, and getting it into awkward corners will test your ingenuity and natural good humor.

it's beautiful

There are lots of wonderful papers around, including stunning designer ranges, hand-printed and historical patterns, as well as fabric wallcoverings such as silk and the rediscovered burlap. A patterned room has a special quality and warmth that cannot be achieved using paint.

it's revealing

Thin paper will show up any small imperfections in the underlying surface and highlight larger ones in full technicolor glory. The wrong pattern and color can make a small room even smaller and a large room difficult to furnish. Wobbly walls and less-than-straight edges will be emphasized by stripes or large patterns.

it's unsuitable

Damp walls are not good for wallpaper unless you can waterproof the surface beforehand with a special sealer. Unless paper is coated the surface will rub off in areas of high wear such as halls and staircases. Furniture will also damage the surface if allowed to come into contact. Porous and noncolorfast papers are not suitable for kitchens or bathrooms where they may come into contact with moisture.

it's easy

New types of papers and adhesives make life easier, and providing you take your time, follow the rules, use the right equipment, and keep calm, there is no reason why you shouldn't derive enormous pleasure from transforming ugly walls into beautiful surfaces, and ordinary rooms into stunning spaces.

types of wallcoverings

Putting wallpaper on the wall can be a lot easier and much more fun than getting it off. New products and methods as well as new, stunning designs have made wallpapering a lot more tempting than it used to be so why not try it.

lining wallpaper

Plain, buff-colored paper used over slightly uneven or impervious surfaces to create a suitable paint surface. Also used underneath expensive wallcoverings.

woodchip wallpaper

Made by sandwiching particles of wood between two layers of paper. Inexpensive and easy to hang, it covers poor plaster and uneven surfaces. Should be painted.

textured-relief wallpapers

Heavily embossed with a variety of patterns, from the traditional designs used extensively in the Victorian and Edwardian eras to more modern and abstract versions. Rarely used on every wall, more often used below a chair rail, or on a ceiling. Always painted. Latex is fine but eggshell and gloss paints are more hardwearing and look more historically accurate. New, simpler, contemporary designs now available that are very different from "authentic" designs.

printed wallpapers

An enormous range of designs and colors from small spriggy flowers to bold geometrics and famous designs from the past. The thickness and quality varies and will be reflected in the price.

prepasted wallpapers

Some wallcoverings are precoated with an adhesive that is activated by soaking in cold water. Specially designed inexpensive plastic trays are available for this process.

coated wallpapers

A thin coating of size is applied to printed papers to create an impervious and washable surface for bathrooms and kitchens. Vinyl wallcoverings consist of a paper or cotton backing with the pattern printed onto a vinyl coating and fused into the surface using heat. These are durable, washable, and colorfast and therefore ideally suited to bathrooms and kitchens. Often sold prepasted.

borders

Borders of varying designs and widths are often intended for use with a coordinating paper but can be used on their own on a painted wall. Some are prepasted.

vintage papers

A number of stores have realized the interest in retro styles and sell rolls of original old wallpaper, especially from the fifties and sixties. It is rare to get any quantity, but these can become a fabulous focus of an interior.

essential equipment

Cutting, pasting, and handling lengths of wallpaper can be awkward and needs a clear space, patience, care, and a sense of humor which you are more likely to retain if you invest in the right equipment.

fold-up pasting table

Cheap and very useful. It is the right size—a little wider than the average roll of paper, and a good working height—slightly higher than a dining room table. It is light and can be moved around easily.

paste brush

Apply adhesive with a large paste brush or wall brush with soft, long bristles. Alternatively use a short-pile paint roller and put the adhesive in the pan.

paperhanger's scissors

These have extra-long blades for straight cuts, but any large pair of sharp scissors will do.

paperhanger's brush

Looking like a wide paintbrush with the handle chopped off, this is used for smoothing the paper onto the wall. The bristles must be soft enough not to damage the surface of the wallpaper, but stiff enough to be poked into corners and force out excess adhesive.

seam roller

Has a small wood or plastic roller which can be run up and down the seams to press down the paper so that it won't lift when dry. Rubber smoothing rollers squeeze trapped air from under the paper. Use a felt roller for more delicate papers. It is probably wise not to use a seam roller on textured paper.

retractable tape measure, plumb bob, and level

Essential for helping you to mark the position of the paper.

wallpaper adhesive

Most adhesives are in the form of powder or flakes ready to mix with water, although ready-mixed pastes are now available.

Standard all-purpose paste is suitable for light- to medium-weight papers but can also be used in a less diluted form for hanging heavy papers.

Heavy-duty or ready-mixed adhesive is used for heavy, embossed papers and paper-backed fabrics.

Fungicidal adhesive prevents the growth of mold behind impervious papers.

Stain-free adhesive is used on delicate papers as conventional paste can stain.

applying wallpaper

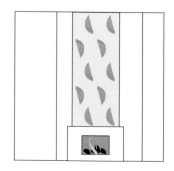

If you are a complete handywoman novice, think carefully before embarking on wallpapering a room. If the room is very large, has high ceilings, is very irregular in shape, or has more than one window and door, it would be wise to call in a professional decorator to do it for you or stick to paint. For your first attempt, why not paper just one feature wall or a narrow chimney breast. This way you avoid corners and having to cut around light switches. Alternatively, start with a room that is very small with no awkward features. Unless you are doing a single wall it is best to stick to patterns that won't look obvious if they don't quite line up.

Many wallpapers come in a fairly standard width and length—approximately 34 feet long and 21 inches wide. To calculate how much you need, measure the wall height from ceiling to baseboard and add 4 inches for trimming to get the length. Work out how many lengths you can get from one roll of wallpaper. Measure around the perimeter of the room (ignoring windows and doors) to find out how many roll widths you will need. Divide this by the number of lengths you can cut from one length to give the number of rolls required. Add to this an allowance for matching up any pattern (the repeat will be written on the label) and add a little more for possible mistakes and accidents. Look out for handy charts for calculating the number of rolls at home improvement and decorating stores.

preparing walls

Prepare walls as for painting but seal newly plastered walls with a proprietary size or diluted wallpaper paste so that the wallpaper will stick. Finish painting ceilings and woodwork before applying wallpaper. Measure the length of wallpaper required adding 4 inches top and bottom, for trimming. Mix up the wallpaper adhesive in a bucket. Cut several lengths, marking the top of each one, and lay them facedown on the pasting table. With the edge of the top length along the side edge of the table, apply paste down the center of the paper and brush out toward the front edge making sure the edges are well covered. Slide the length across to the back edge of the table and brush on more adhesive toward that edge, making sure that edge is also well covered. Fold the pasted paper over onto itself, then slide the paper along the table and repeat the process until the whole length is pasted.

things with string

To prevent the ends of cut lengths curling and getting in the way, tuck them behind a length of string tied around the legs of the pasting table. Similarly, tie a piece of string across the middle of the paste bucket to rest the pasting brush on.

papering a room

If possible, start on a blank wall with no windows or doors. Beginning in one corner, work away from the window so you are not working in your own light. Measuring from the corner, use a plumb bob or carpenter's level to mark a plumb line on the wall that is $1/2$ inch less than the width of the roll (to allow for an overlap around the corner). Leaving the bottom half folded for easier handling, place the top of the pasted strip on the wall allowing the paper to overlap onto the ceiling by approximately 2 inches and slide it so that it aligns with the marked line. Use the paperhanger's brush to brush the paper onto the wall. Use gentle strokes and work from the middle outward to squeeze out trapped air and excess adhesive. Run the tip of a scissor blade along the paper where it joins the ceiling, peel the paper away, cut off the excess, then brush the paper back onto the wall. Unfold the rest of the strip and brush the rest of the paper onto the wall (making sure you push the paper into the corner) until you reach the baseboard where you trim as above. Wipe away excess adhesive as you go using a damp cloth.

Turn a corner by marking another line so that the paper covers the overlap. When you reach a door or window frame allow the length of wallpaper to fall across the door or window and make a diagonal cut. Brush the paper into place along the side of the woodwork, then score with scissors, and trim leaving $1/2$ inch along the top edge for the piece above the frame and brush back. Brush down remaining paper above the door and trim along the top of the frame as before.

papering techniques

starting in a corner

Brush seams to remove excess adhesive and finish with a seam roller.

papering around a window

For a neat edge around a window recess, paper the top of the recess separately, paper over the overlap, and cut along the edge.

papering around a door

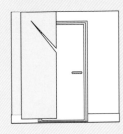

Make a diagonal cut, trim, brush into place around the frame, and trim off any excess.

papering around a radiator and a light switch

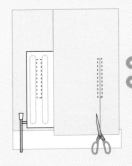
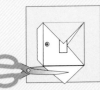

Mark position of radiator bracket and cut from the bottom. Push paper into position around bracket using a long-handled brush. Trim the diagonal cuts, unscrew the light switch, tuck paper behind, and screw back into postion.

wallpaper projects

Wallpaper is back in fashion with new chic designs by established designers as well as a revival in nostalgic pretty prints. Plain painted walls can complement every interior style but wallpaper can be used for historic authenticity, as a fashion statement, or to add a touch of luxury or indulgent femininity.

main feature

Papering a single wall is not only easier to do but also an opportunity to be adventurous. Choose a very bold or dramatic print that would otherwise swamp the room. Use it to set a style, a theme, or just a color story.

inside job

If you are a firm fan of plain walls but love wallpaper designs, put some on the inside of a closet. Surround your blouses with blousy roses, discipline your suits with stripes, or cheer up your little black dresses with jazzy prints. Line drawers and boxes with pretty papers to keep delicate fabrics safe and make the contents feel loved.

indulge

Give in to your innermost desires and paper a
bedroom in pretty roses—you know you want to.
Use two or three different patterns in the same
colorway or use the same pattern in different
colors. Do the ceiling, too. And put up matching
curtains if you dare. Convert a small dark room
into a salon with deep-colored silky wallcoverings
and a few gold patterns. Go hippy with a riot of
patterns in bright colors or fill the bathroom with
ships and seagulls.

a bit of art

Create large modern paintings by pasting papers
onto plywood "canvases." Prop them against plain
walls or hang them gallery-style. A good way of
appreciating those vintage panels you picked up
from the retro shop. Be really ironic and put them in
fancy gold frames.

essential points about tiles

Tiles give a crisp, clean, and efficient finish in a kitchen or bathroom where their hard surface is practical, water-resistant, and easy to clean. Their regular, even shape and finish makes them perfect for an architectural, minimal look while chunky and hand-painted tiles in glowing colors can be used to add warmth and character in any room.

they are practical...
Tiles are hard-wearing, waterproof, and easy to clean, making them ideal for bathrooms, showers, kitchens, and utility rooms.

they are easy to cut...
Making straight cuts on thin ceramic wall tiles is surprisingly easy using tile cutters and tile nippers, and easier still with a platform cutter.

they are versatile...
Can be used on walls and floors but also on tables and countertops. Their color and finish can set the look from hard-edged modern to handmade ethnic.

they look good...
Crisp, clean, smooth, and cool for a modern look. Soft, mat, warm, and colorful for traditional or country style. Perfect when plain but pretty when patterned.

they are difficult to cut...
Curves must be cut neatly with a tile saw which is difficult for an amateur. Thicker tiles need to be cut with a special cutter, heavy-duty platform cutter, or a power wet saw.

they are easy to keep clean...
Their hard surface repels dirt and any splashes can be wiped off with a damp cloth.

they look dreadful...
The uniformity of tiles emphasizes bad workmanship, but even if the tiles have been put up beautifully they will never look good if the color or pattern is not to your taste.

they need cleaning often...
Clean tiles regularly, especially in a shower where a buildup of soap will coat the tiles with a dull, scummy film.

types of tiles

There are now lots of specialist tile shops—have a good browse and be inspired!

ceramic tiles

Available in a variety of shapes and sizes, plain and patterned, shiny or mat. Most are square and the most common sizes are 4 inches and 6 inches. Larger sizes and rectangular, octagonal, and interlocking shapes are also available.

glazed tiles

Have a hard shiny coating of glaze which is waterproof and very durable.

unglazed tiles

Have a duller, mat finish and may need to be sealed to reduce porosity.

industrially produced tiles

Usually quite thin and therefore easy to cut. Their machine-made precision means the thickness, surface finish, color, and pattern is uniform and therefore they are easy to install.

handmade tiles

More irregular in shape and they are usually thicker than machine-made tiles. The color and finish will vary and patterns will be less precise which gives them more "character."

mosaic tiles

Small and give a different sort of look. Laying them individually would be very time-consuming so they are either attached to mesh backing which remains in place after applying, or a paper covering which is removed once they are in place.

curved tiles

Most tiles sold now have straight edges on all sides but some have one curved, finished edge for neater edges on window sills and panels.

narrow border tiles

There are a number of narrow border tiles, many of them decorative and some with relief patterns. Small thin pencil tiles are available for edging.

mirror tiles

Fixed with self-adhesive pads (usually included with the tile) and are butted together with no gaps.

other materials

Most tiles are ceramic, but the popularity of stone and slate for floors has led to the development of thinner versions for walls. As a natural material they are not easy to cut and are best left to expert tilers.

equipment

For a professional finish, make the most of the many new products for cutting and applying.

platform or tile cutter

Used to cut tiles in half. A platform cutter is easier and safer to use than a tile cutter, with which you have to score and snap by hand.

tile nippers

Pincers used to cut narrow strips, small notches, and corners.

tile saw

Used for cutting out curved shapes when fitting tiles around pipes, etc.

metal file, tile sander, and oiled slip stone

Used to smooth down cut edges.

tile adhesive

Usually sold ready-mixed and most are water-resistant.

spacers

Guides for spacing tiles accurately.

grout

Fills gaps between tiles. Supplied in powder form to be mixed with water. Heat-resistant versions for kitchens and epoxy-based versions for germ-free countertops are available.

plastic edging strip

Makes corners and edges of tiling neater; protects them from chips.

preparing walls for tiling

Before deciding to try your hand at tiling look carefully at the area to be tiled. If possible, avoid having to tile around windows, fixtures, pipes, and awkward recesses. Don't be too ambitious; stick to small areas such as behind a countertop or a sink. Industrially produced tiles will be easier to use as they are uniform in size and shape and are not too thick. However, as handmade tiles are irregular in shape, slightly irregular spacing and an uneven surface will not show too much!

how many tiles?

It is not too difficult to calculate the number of tiles needed. Work out how many of your chosen tiles will be needed for the height and the width of the area to be covered. Multiply the two figures and add 10 percent (perhaps 15 percent for beginners) for breakages and mistakes.

preparing surfaces

Tiles can be stuck to most surfaces as long as they are flat, clean, and dry, with no loose paint, plaster, or debris. New plaster should be left for several weeks in order to dry out properly. Don't tile over wallpaper. Taking off old tiles is a messy and laborious business, but fortunately you can tile on top. Scrape out any loose grout, stick down any loose tiles, and fill any big gaps with patching compound. Prepare unstable surfaces with a coat of all-purpose sealer but make sure it is the waterproof variety.

marking out

Make a tiling gauge by laying out a row of tiles with spacers in between each one and carefully marking the position of each tile on a long (straight) piece of 2-inch wide thin softwood. Use this to plan where the tiles should go. The layout needs to be worked out carefully so that the amount of cutting is kept to a minimum, so stick to whole tiles wherever possible. If the tiles span the whole wall, don't start at one side as walls are rarely straight and you may end up with gaps that are impossible to fill in. Position the first whole tile away from the edge and check each side to make sure that the cut tiles at either edge are of roughly even width—draw a vertical line down the center and work out from this.

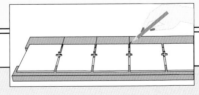

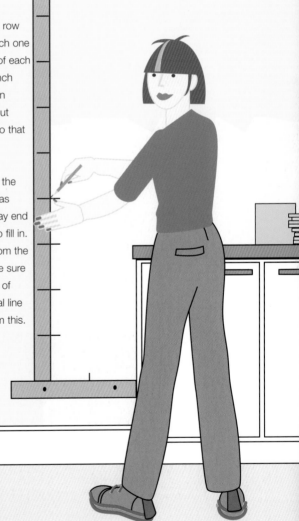

applying tiles

The most difficult part of tiling is cutting them to fit around objects and into corners. However, the availability of good, reasonably priced tile cutters and a few tips will make this a less daunting prospect.

simple tiling techniques

For backsplashes or small panels, choose a depth based on numbers of whole tiles so that you don't have to cut the bottom row. Mark the first horizontal row of tiles, using a level to make sure they are straight. For extra accuracy and easy positioning, secure level support boards along the side and bottom against which the tiles can be placed.

Apply adhesive to the wall using a notched trowel to make it easier to position and bed the tile. Do no more than 1 square yard at a time to avoid the adhesive drying out. Position the first tile in the corner formed by the two support boards if you are using them.

Always start with a whole tile. Press the tile into place until it feels firm. Using spacers as you go, continue working in rows, adding adhesive as required and wiping away excess with a damp sponge. Allow 12 hours before removing the support boards. Finish by filling in with cut tiles. Make sure crosshead spacers do not protrude above the surface or they will stick out above the grout.

tile projects

mind the gap

Use different colored grout to give an unexpected or ultra-smart effect. Use gray with white tiles, or vice versa, for a subtler look. Using a similar color grout and tiles will make the gaps "disappear" while a contrasting color with darker tones will look dramatic.

color theory

For subtle variation, use two close tones in alternating rows or in a checkerboard pattern. Or be very bold and use contrasting colors. Handmade tiles give a wonderful melange of color—look out for warm Provençal yellows and Moroccan tiles in vibrant turquoise.

reflected glory

Use mirror tiles in a bathroom for an all-round view or tile a panel or narrow strip in a bedroom or dressing room. Reflect light into a dark passageway with a strategically placed panel of mirror tiles.

shaping up

Rectangular tiles are very chic. Use them lengthwise, laid in a brick-like pattern, or try them different ways up for something completely different. Make thin stripes across or down unexciting walls.

border control

Add interest with a row of tiles in a contrasting color or texture along the top and sides of a tiled panel. Narrow rectangular tiles in plain colors are smart, and a single row of pencil tiles in the same color will look minimal.

table talk

Cheer up a dull table or cabinet top with a brightly colored tiled top (use a flexible adhesive and grout). Use any bits of broken tile if you don't want to buy new especially for this and create a mad mosaic. Place a collection of loose tiles in the center of a dinner table for added decoration and a perfect surface for hot dishes.

mixing it

Go wild with mixed colors and patterns. Use rough or old tiles picked up from flea markets to add a surprise element to plain walls or to design a whole patchwork wall.

tiling techniques

tiling a simple backsplash

Measure and mark the position of the tiles and, using a level board as a guide, work in rows starting in a top corner.

When tiling in a recess or lining the tiles up exactly with the edge of cabinets mark the center line and work out to the edges.

tiling behind cabinets

For tiled areas that extend beyond and around cabinets, place a level board along the side and one along the line of the bottom of the lowest whole tile. Place the first tile where these strips join.

Take away the boards before measuring, cutting, and positioning the final edge tiles.

cutting and fitting edge tiles

Fit edge tiles after all the whole tiles have been put on and mark each one individually as the edges of the wall may not be straight. To work out the size, place a tile face down, on top of the neighboring tile and against the edge of the wall or baseboard. Mark along the edge of the tile, not forgetting to make an allowance for the spacing. Spread adhesive on the back of each filler tile and press into position.

grouting tiles

Allow 24 hours for the adhesive to harden. Using a rubber-bladed spreader or a piece of dense foam sponge, spread grout in all directions forcing it into all the gaps. Wipe grout from the surface of the tiles using a barely damp sponge. When the grout has dried polish the tiles with a dry cloth.

finishing off

Unless you have used tiles with a curved edge, grout around exposed edges to form a smooth joint with the wall.

applying mosaic tiles

Mosaic tiles are usually supplied in sheets on a mesh backing or with a facing paper which is removed after application. Use the same adhesives and grouting as standard tiles but make sure that the gap left around each set of tiles is the same as the gap between the individual tiles. In order to make sure the tiles are bedded properly, apply pressure with a piece of board covered in a soft material such as carpet, and tap gently with a wooden mallet. Fill in the margins by cutting strips, or single tiles from the sheet using tile nippers to cut to size.

sealing gaps and edges

If the tiles are immediately above a sink or bathtub don't grout the adjacent seal. Instead fill it with flexible silicone caulk. This is sold in plastic tubes with a pointed nozzle; some need to be used with a caulk gun but others can be squeezed by hand. Before application make sure the surface is dry and wipe with denatured alcohol to get rid of any grease. Squeeze an even bead of caulk along the joint. It takes a steady hand and steady pressure to get a good finish; do it all in one movement as joints will show. A strip of masking tape will help get a straight edge. Smooth the surface with a finger dipped in a 50/50 solution of water and dishwashing liquid.

tiling around an electrical outlet

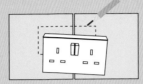 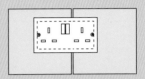

Unscrew the outlet cover, postion tile, and mark position of outlet allowing for an overlap, but making sure the screw holes are not covered. Screw cover back on after grouting is finished and set.

cutting an edge tile

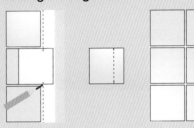

Place a whole tile upside down on top of a tile in the last row of whole, fixed tiles and position it against the finished edge. Allowing for the space between the tiles and, if necessary, grouting between the edge of the wall or baseboard, mark the edge of the tile and cut to size.

grouting tiles

Spread grout in all directions making sure to cover any spacers. After it has dried wipe off any remaining grout with a soft, dry cloth.

applying mosaic tiles

  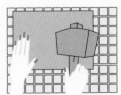

A mesh backing or facing paper mak(easier. Keep the spaces between the as the space between individual tiles. Use a carpet covered pad and a wooden mallet to bed the tiles into the adhesive.

off-the-rack or tailor-made

taking on self-assembly or homemade furniture

Now that you have a neat, freshly decorated interior, the fun can really start. You will, of course, have sorted out your clutter so only the items that are good, useful, or well-loved remain, so now comes the opportunity to organize and arrange your possessions to transform your living space into a visually pleasing, convenient, and comfortable environment. Create your own personal style using a combination of color, simple home improvement and a few new purchases. Fortunately there is a wonderful choice of products on the market and even if your budget is modest it is still possible to buy simple, well-designed furniture and furnishings to make your home stunning and stylish or just peaceful and calm, according to your personality or lifestyle.

The design, choice, and quality of self-assembly furniture has never been better. Despite the often mystifying assembly instructions, patience and a positive attitude will eventually be rewarded with a good-looking, useful item to enhance your home.

The problem of finding somewhere to store or display all your possessions is often solved by the ever-useful shelf. The ability to put up shelves is a skill no self-respecting, modern, emancipated female should be without. Adding shelves in cabinets, closets, and alcoves, too, will maximize the use of space and enable you

to store things efficiently or display them beautifully.

Making your own furniture may require advanced carpentry skills but a trip to a home improvement store can inspire innovative, easy-to-make ideas. Invest in castors and allow your imagination to run away by fixing them to plywood or ready-made doors to make a roll-along coffee table or a bed base.

The variety of curtain rods, wires, and fixtures has made covering windows a lot more straightforward, and the fashion for simple panels and shades requires only straight lines and basic sewing skills. The huge range of ready-made roll-down shades require only the use of a power drill and a screwdriver to install and give a room a clean, modern feel. If you are feeling adventurous, employ your knowledge of attaching hinges and support boards to make your own made-to-measure shutters.

Use your decorating skills to cheer up old unsightly furniture and bring it into line with the rest of the decor or to give that self-assembly pack a professional finish. Scour the secondhand furniture and antique stores for solid but quirky items, getting out your toolbox to carry out a little repair and restoration or turn them into something completely different with the addition of a few odds and ends and a dash of inventiveness.

getting it together

Knowing that you can drop in at the local furniture store, pick up enough items to fill a small house, and fit it all in your car is one of the great pleasures of the modern age. Unfortunately, putting together self-assembly furniture has become one of the greatest challenges, but it can be done. If you adopt a positive, realistic approach, there is no reason why putting together a dresser or bookcase should not be an enjoyable task and even the highlight of your week.

take your time

The first rule is to allow plenty of time. It always takes longer than you think. Even though you cannot wait to transform the drawing on that slim box of parts into its three-dimensional form, don't think that you can do it in those couple of hours between bringing it home and going out for the evening. Treat it as a pleasurable activity and plan a day around it: get in plenty of snacks, but avoid alcohol—save that for the celebration of a job well done or, in extreme circumstances, a good way of forgetting. Don't attempt it if you are feeling grumpy, and don't invite lots of people to help. Do get one other person to help, as two sets of arms and hands can be useful.

room for maneuver

Choose where the assembly will take place. Allow plenty of space, but if the piece of furniture is very large make sure you will be able to get it into the room it is destined for. Make sure you have the right tools. Some will be included with the kit, but you may need screwdrivers, wrenches and, if it is a particularly adventurous purchase, clamps.

take a count

Unpack carefully. Avoid tearing the cardboard box—keep it, open it out, and use it to work on. It will protect the parts, and the floor, from accidental scratches. Examine all the pieces for damage. If they are damaged, pack it all up again and take it back—annoying, but worth it in the end. If you are lucky there will be a list of components and instructions so you can check everything is there. Identify each piece and make sure they look like those in the diagram. Make sure you understand what each piece is and what it is for. Count the screws, bolts,

and fixings and make sure the numbers correspond with the numbers stated on the instructions. Sometimes extra screws are included—make sure you are aware of this in order to avoid the panic induced by the sight of two large screws glinting ominously alongside an apparently fully assembled piece of furniture.

stick to the plan

Lay everything out. Some pieces may look similar, so to make sure you don't end up with something that is upside down or inside out, mark and identify each piece with useful phrases such as "this way up" written on pieces of paper secured with removable tape. Next, follow the instructions. This sounds obvious and easy, but unfortunately isn't always the case. Some instruction sheets are notable by their absence while others require either a lot of imagination, the ability to speak a foreign language, or an advanced qualification in technical drawing. Fortunately, things have improved and most good-quality self-assembly furniture comes with a fairly clear guide—or even a video! Even

if you think you know better, do things in the order it says—there is a usually a good reason. It is best to obey instructions otherwise you may be forced to take everything apart again just to fix one drawer runner or hinge.

don't panic

If things don't seem to be going too well, keep calm. Take a break and have a snack while you look through the instructions again. Don't force anything or assume that because holes nearly correspond they are the right ones in the right place. It is tempting to assume that a hole has been drilled in the wrong place but computerized mass production means that unless the robots were out for revenge, it is unlikely that a hole has been made where it shouldn't. However, manufacturing errors do occur, so if things don't make sense it is worth calling the store where you bought it to check if they have had similar complaints. Mostly, things start to fit together nicely but be careful not to get carried away and ruin things by rushing. Check regularly that nothing has been left out and everything is the right way

round and the right way up. Don't tighten every screw or bolt immediately, in case you need to allow for some adjustment. Also, the instructions may specify in which order everything should be tightened.

final analysis

If at any time during the proceedings, the object growing in front of you ceases to resemble the drawing on the box or instructions, or the photograph in the catalog, then don't panic. Sometimes, the same instructions are used to cover a range of different designs. This is because the basic components are similar, and the differences are in details such as color, material, or trimmings. It could be, however, that you have made a minor, or even major, mistake in your assembly. Go back to the instructions and, if necessary, take it all apart and start again, in which case, for the benefit of your own emotional state and to protect the potential piece of furniture, walk away from it for a while and start again when you are feeling better. If you still can't work it out, pack it all away neatly and phone a friend.

shelves made easy

Shelves are incredibly useful, and in even the most well-equipped home there is always room for at least one more. Open shelves turn storage into display and can become an important component, or even the centerpiece, of an interior.

shelving considerations

The shelving system you choose will depend on the state of the wall on which you want your shelves and what you want to store. Partition walls will not be able to support heavy shelves or heavy loads unless you are able to screw the supports or brackets into the wooden studs. The walls of old properties may be too soft and crumbly to hold screws securely and drilling into stone is not easy. Some properties have concrete walls which require a very powerful drill for even the smallest jobs. If drilling into the wall is not an option, you may decide to solve your shelving requirements with a free-standing system.

Aesthetics are also important— imaginative materials can turn simple components into a style statement. Shelves are most often made of wood, since it is easy to cut to size and is available in many varieties, but glass and metal can also be used. Shelves are supported and fixed to the wall in a variety of ways including brackets, support boards, slotted uprights, and dowels. It is easy to assume that buying brackets and shelves separately is cheaper, but although the individual components are not expensive the combined cost can be higher than the price of a bookcase or ready-packaged system, so work it out before making a final decision.

shelving materials

Home improvement stores sell ready-made shelving in a variety of lengths, widths, and finishes and will often cut specified lengths free of charge. Wooden shelves left bare need treating and sealing to prevent them from drying out and distorting, and if they are to be painted they will need priming first.

solid wood

Softwoods such as pine are relatively inexpensive and can be stained and sealed or painted.

hardwood

Available from lumberyards, hardwoods such as oak and beech look wonderful but are more expensive and heavier than other shelving materials.

laminated solid wood

Strips or blocks of solid wood glued together to form a knot-free surface suitable for sealing or painting.

plywood

Thin layers of wood sandwiched together and glued into sheets. Good for shelves, but should be cut by machine and the edges will need careful finishing.

laminated boards

Particleboard covered with laminate or veneer. Light, convenient, and inexpensive.

metal

Stainless steel and wire mesh are great shelving materials, but buy ready-cut and finished as they are difficult to work with.

glass

Use toughened glass and always get it cut and finished by a glass supplier.

off-the-rack shelving systems

Look out for ready-made shelves at home improvement stores. With some shelving systems the shelves are often sold separately and can be used for convenience or to give a more prosaic shelving system a smarter look. There are a number of flexible shelving systems on the market which vary in price and complexity. The simplest consist of narrow metal uprights with slots or a single groove along their whole length into which purpose-made metal brackets are fitted. The choice of positions is wide and the brackets can be moved easily to adjust the height of the shelves.

off-the-shelf shelves

A variety of "ready-to-hang" shelves are available. Some incorporate extras such as hanging rails, plate racks, etc., while others are plain but made from more unusual materials such as wire mesh, stainless steel, or plastic—materials that an amateur would have difficulty working with. Most can be fixed directly to the wall with screws (which are often included, along with wall anchors) so require nothing more than a drill and a level to put them up.

The floating shelf, one of the most popular of the "ready-to-hang" varieties, is a box-like construction with a support board and bolt system which is concealed within the construction so that the shelf "floats" with no visible means of support. These look very smart and "architectural" and can be surprisingly inexpensive. Putting them up involves screwing the support board to the wall and securing the shelf to the board from underneath.

free-standing shelving

There are a variety of free-standing shelving systems, from very inexpensive wooden or metal units for garage or utility room storage to smarter combinations using high-quality materials. Most consist of uprights and shelves in a choice of height, width, and depth and are usually very easy to assemble.

They are ideal if your walls are not suitable for fixing into, or you don't want or are not allowed to drill into them. Easy to take down and reassemble in a different position according to need or whim, they can also be used as room dividers. Inexpensive wooden systems are perfect as a temporary storage solution to keep everything under control while you plan more permanent or sophisticated fixtures, but they can also be smartened up with stain or paint to suit the decor.

brackets

Simple brackets are screwed to the wall individually. The size and number of brackets required will depend on the length, depth, and width of the shelf and its load-bearing requirements.

Pressed steel brackets are inexpensive and can look very chic in a "loft" sort of way. Look out for smarter designs in stainless steel and curved plywood. Inexpensive brackets are sold singly but the more expensive versions are often sold in pairs.

Brackets are ideal for a single shelf—use large, chunky brackets and a slab of wood as a feature, or use several brackets to support a long shelf which could even extend around the whole room.

Systems using brackets that slot into a metal upright, which is screwed into the wall, are adjustable and involve less drilling.

quick tips

putting up shelves

double measure

When putting up shelves inside alcoves take measurements at the back, the front, and all the way down as the walls are rarely true. Unless you want an exact fit, get all the shelves cut to the smallest measurement.

weight watching

To ensure good support when putting shelves on brackets, make sure there is sufficient overhang each side of the brackets. The amount will depend on the thickness of the shelf and the weight of the load. Books are heavy and therefore you may need extra brackets and stout shelves to avoid sag or collapse. Most brackets have holes for screwing the bracket to the underside of the shelf. This strengthens the fixture and prevents the shelf from tipping or sliding.

on the level

Always use a level for marking and positioning shelves so that they are level. Sloping walls and ceiling may make the shelf look "out" but lining up with anything other than the true horizontal and vertical will lead to problems that are structural as well as visual.

You can never have too many shelves so put one up today!

shelves with brackets

The shelf is positioned so it overhangs the brackets at each end but will sag if either the brackets are too far apart or the shelf material is too thin or weak to support sufficient weight. The bracket should span nearly the whole depth of the shelf, and for heavy loads, the part of the bracket that fixes to the wall needs to be long enough to provide good support.

Mark the position of the shelf on the wall then work out the positions of the brackets allowing for the overhang. If you are using more than two brackets, space them evenly along the length of the shelf, measuring from the center for accuracy. Hold one bracket to the wall using a level to ensure it is straight and mark the positions of the holes. Drill the holes and screw the bracket to the wall. Hold the next bracket against the wall on its marked position. If you are using more than two brackets, do the end ones first. Place the shelf across both brackets, place a level on the shelf and adjust the position of the bracket until the shelf is level. Mark the position of the holes and secure as before.

adjustable shelving systems

To work out where the uprights need to be positioned, secure the first upright to the wall with the top screw only. Using a level to ensure it is vertical, mark the positions of the other screws (see fig. 1). Next screw the first upright to the wall with the required number of screws. Insert a bracket near the top of the fixed upright and another in the corresponding position on the second unfixed upright. Hold it where it is to be fixed to the wall. Place a shelf across the brackets and, using a level, move the upright to the correct position, and mark the top hole. Then secure as before (see fig. 2).

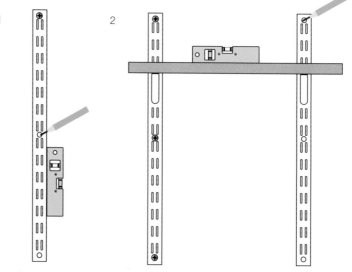

shelves for alcoves

shelves with side supports

Where shelves span the entire area between two walls—such as in an alcove—they can be supported on boards screwed to the side walls. As the support is at the ends only, it is important to use a sufficiently strong shelf so it won't sag. The support board is cut shorter than the shelf and the front edge is cut at an angle so it is less visible. For wide spans and heavy loads, extra support can be provided by adding another board along the back, or a lipping of wood attached to the front edge of the shelf and board, in which case the support board spans the full depth of the shelf.

Cut support boards to the required length, sand the edges, and angle the ends if they will show. Drill clearance holes right through, and countersink. Work out the position of each shelf and mark the position of the support boards on one wall only. Starting at the top, screw on the first board (see page 32), then place the shelf in position supported on the fixed board and the unfixed board held up on the other side. When you are satisfied the shelf is level, mark the position of the board with a pencil or with a bradawl poked through pre-drilled holes.

An alternative to support boards are extruded aluminum supports, which will usually be cut the full depth of the shelf and therefore be visible at the front giving a neat, "modern" feel. The suitability for heavy loads will vary according to the design and make.

angled supports

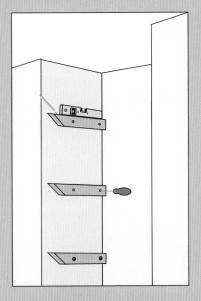

Take the support boards with clearance holes and, with a bradawl, mark the positions according to the spacing you require between each shelf. Screw the boards to one side of the alcove only.

Place a loose shelf on the fixed support boards and, using a level to make sure the shelf is level, mark the position of the opposite boards.

fascia shelving

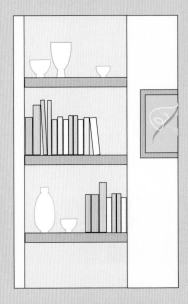

For a neat look, fix a fascia along the front of shelves. Measure accurately the alcove depth, then cut the support boards and shelves short of the outside edge so when the fascia is added it is flush with the wall.

Attach the fascia with long brads, tapping them well in so they can be concealed by filler before sealing or painting.

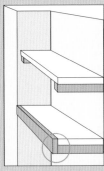

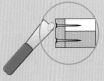

step 1 Use six castors for strength, mark their position accurately, and don't put them too near the edges.

step 2 Screw the castors into position and check that they move freely and the base is level. If the castor stem or screw is deeper than the base, screw blocks of wood to the base first.

daybed on castors

Furniture that is moveable is convenient and practical as well as fun. Castors can be fixed to solid wood and laminated boards to make coffee tables and TV trolleys, or attached to boxes and baskets for versatile storage space. A wide range of castor sizes is available. Some are fixed by a flat plate with screw holes, but many have a stem that screws or slots into a sleeve that is fitted into a drilled hole. Some have brackets to prevent an item rolling away at an inopportune moment.

A good-looking, strong daybed is simple to make using robust castors screwed to a flat, solid-core fire-resistant door, which is strong enough to withstand a heavy weight and thick enough to hold the castors securely. Choose swivel-type castors that have a reasonably large wheel and preferably a rubber tire.

castors Some castors have a flat plate which is screwed directly onto the base, while others have a stem which requires a pre-drilled hole.

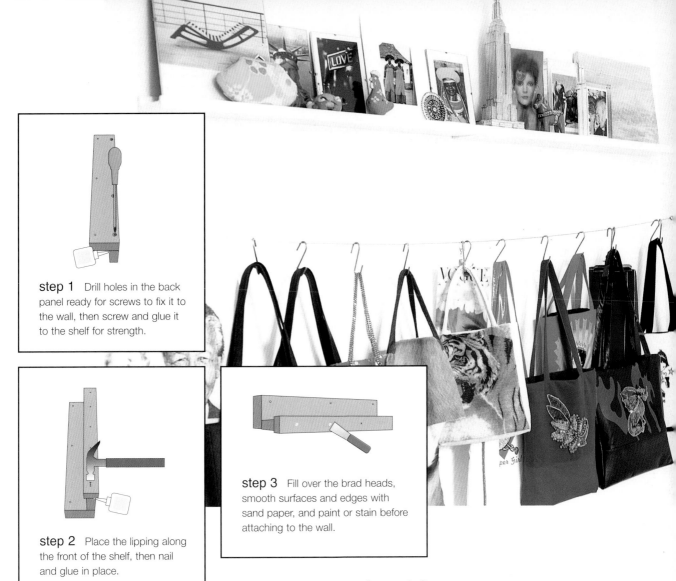

step 1   Drill holes in the back panel ready for screws to fix it to the wall, then screw and glue it to the shelf for strength.

step 2   Place the lipping along the front of the shelf, then nail and glue in place.

step 3   Fill over the brad heads, smooth surfaces and edges with sand paper, and paint or stain before attaching to the wall.

picture shelf

Picture shelves allow you to change the arrangement of favorite artworks without peppering the wall with holes. Large pictures look stunning displayed in this way, but the shelf will need to be strong and well supported. A securely anchored lipping or fascia must be provided to prevent the pictures from sliding off.

Cut three pieces of wood—a back panel, a shelf, and front lipping. The dimensions of the shelf and the materials depend on the size and weight of the pictures. Using boards makes the job simpler. For a shelf strong enough to hold pictures in frames, use a back that is no less than $3/4$ inch thick and 4–5 inches wide. Make the shelf slightly narrower than the back and choose a fascia that overlaps both edges of the shelf providing extra structural strength as well as a ledge against which the pictures can rest.

10 ways with windows

How you treat your windows sets the scene, and the standard, for the rest of the room. Contemporary interiors maximize the impact of light and leave windows uncovered and uncluttered with the use of shades, Venetian blinds, shutters, and simple panels.

bare if you dare

If you like the pared-down look (and are not overlooked), leave your windows unadorned. If you are overlooked and value your privacy, use etched glass or plastic film.

straight and narrow

Gathers are out. The newest curtains are simple panels, just a bit wider than the window, and hang straight from ungathered tops.

venetian splendor

Slatted blinds in wood or metal look smart and very architectural. They can be adjusted to filter the light or block out the night, and pulled up out of the way in the day.

pole position

Hang curtains, panels, dhurries, or throws from simple poles. Attach them with rings, ties, loops, clips, or even safety pins. Keep it plain or add fancy finials for a little extravagance.

rings and things

Rods and wires are popular, so rings are the thing. Choose from chunky wood, dull metal, shiny brass, cool steel, and practical plastic. Keep tabs or ties on simple panels and try something out with clip-on rings or stationery grips. Eyelets are cool and kitchen hooks are useful, too.

the shutters are up

If you are fortunate enough to have original, old shutters you will know how they enhance the character of a home and allow you to control the light and the view. Ultra-modern shutters are perfectly plain, while slatted versions look pleasingly European or a little Colonial.

only natural

Bamboo and paper, unbleached cottons, coarse and crisp linens, hairy tweeds, felted wools, and plain calico are naturally friendly (and terribly trendy).

great lengths

Cropped drapes are all the rage. No need to have them touching the sills or hovering just above the carpet; let them hang out halfway between the window ledge and the floor.

along the wires

Metal tension wires are hardly visible and perfect for pared-down interiors. Use fine rings or special hooks to hang simple fabric, or perhaps paper panels.

on the rails

Sometimes good old curtain rail is the best for the job. It can bend around bays and hide behind valances, and some have cords for effortless pulling. One type of rail has the track and gliders cunningly concealed inside a metal casing that looks like a rod.

guide to drapes, shades, and shutters

Most drape fixtures involve a rod or track fitted into, and supported by, brackets that are anchored to the wall or window frame with screws. Make sure the wall is suitable and that the screws are secured firmly—the weight of the drapes plus the action of opening and closing them puts quite a strain on the fixings. If the wall is not suitable for screwing into you can screw directly into the window trim—but check that it is sound—and don't deface a beautiful window. Alternatively, put up a support board and screw the brackets to this.

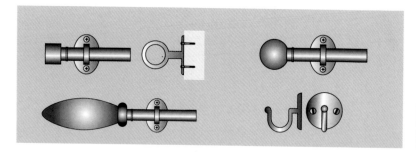

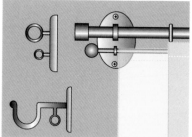

rods and finials

Rods are very popular and very easy to put up. Available in a wide range of lengths, thicknesses, materials and finishes, they can be cut to size and corner sections are available for bay windows. The rods are supported by brackets or sockets screwed to the wall. Finials are usually placed on the ends of the rod as a form of decoration and to stop the rod slipping out of the bracket.

For small windows, one length of rod and two brackets will be enough. For wide spans, a third bracket in the middle is necessary to stop a single rod from sagging or to hide and support a join between two rods. Thicker rods and extra brackets may be necessary if the drapes are very heavy.

doubles

Brackets that carry two rods, or a rod and a wire, and rails that incorporate two tracks are neat ways of hanging two sets of window coverings.

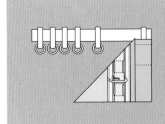

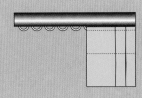

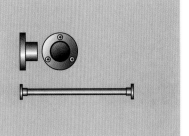

rails

Rails are traditional supports for drapes. The drape is attached by hooks to gliders that move freely along the rail. The cheapest are simple strips of bendy plastic that fit into brackets screwed to the wall or the window frame and can be installed by amateurs. Smarter, more sophisticated versions are made from strong plastic or metal and the gliders are hidden behind a plain strip of aluminum or stainless steel. Some have the rail and gliders hidden within a casing. Rails can go around bends and corners and, as the brackets do not obstruct the rail, the drapes can be pulled right back. Also, the rails can overlap so that the drapes close properly to keep out light and drafts.

sockets

Where a rod spans the whole length between two walls, metal and wooden sockets that are fixed to the side walls provide a neat alternative to brackets. Ideal for inside window recesses and can also be used for shower curtains.

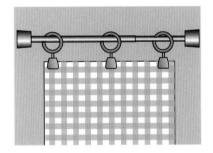

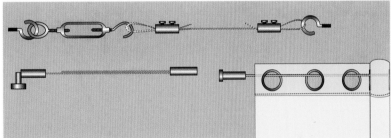

plastic telescopic rods

These are useful for hanging lightweight fabrics, such as sheers, which can be threaded on rather than attached with clips or rings.

telescopic rods

Cafe rods are slim poles, often telescopic, intended for use with a half height "cafe" curtain, which can be attached with rings, clips, or threaded onto the rod.

wires and cables

Wires and cables are becoming popular for hanging lightweight drapes or panels which are hung using eyelets, rings, or clips. The cable must be very taut and is stretched between hooks or brackets with the use of tensioners.

Commercially produced systems include tensioners within neat bracket mechanisms, but you can also make your own with cable grips, tensioners, and wire available at most home improvement stores.

Wires are often incorporated into double hanging systems along with a rod or rail.

mind the gap

Place the brackets far enough from the window casing to allow the drapes to be pulled right back from the window. Also, some rings take up a large amount of space.

The top of the drapes will hang a little below the rod so make sure the pole is high enough above the window trim so that the window and trim are covered.

When the rod is supported on a center bracket the drapes won't quite close. Try putting the last ring a little way from the edge of the drape so that there is a small overlap. If the drape material is floppy, sew or insert some form of stiffening (a paperclip might do), to keep the edge straight.

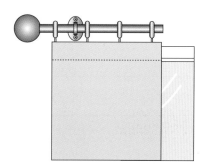

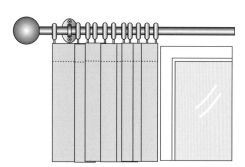

hanging drapes

Attaching drapes to a rod or rail can be done in a variety of ways, some of them traditional and others inventive and unusual. Hooks, rings, and other fastenings are often included with prepacked rails and rods, but many can be bought separately enabling you to create your own combinations to suit specific requirements and offering the opportunity for a little mix-and-match madness.

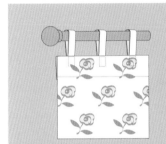

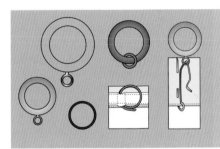

rings

Available in a variety of sizes and materials, from old-fashioned thin metal rings to flat stainless steel versions. Some have eyes, loops, or hooks for attaching the drape.

fabric tabs

Used to attach a drape directly on to a rod or hook. Use cords and ribbons for something different. Look for separate tabs made from stiff materials which are fixed to the drapes through eyelets.

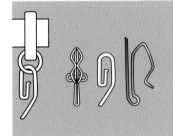

hooks

Designed to slot through a heading tape, hooks won't be seen. Plastic hooks are cheap and functional; metal ones are stronger. Use the old-fashioned variety for a retro look.

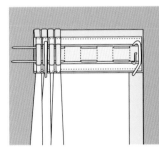

heading tapes

Sewn to the top edge of the drapes to provide slots for hooks and cords for gathering. Available with stiffening for deep pleated headings or double rows of slots for attaching linings.

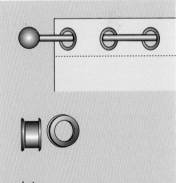

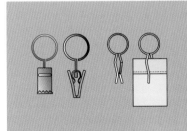

clips

Often referred to as "cafe clips" consisting of a ring or hook incorporating a clip which grips the curtain or drape. Mostly used for lightweight fabrics.

eyelets

Bought as kits with tools for fixing, they are fitted at the top of a curtain and threaded directly onto rods, cables, or hooks. Available in large sizes suitable for heavier fabrics.

window shades and blinds

Window shades and blinds have traditionally been used in kitchens and bathrooms where curtains would be impractical, but with the vogue for simple, pared-down interiors they are now widely used for all rooms. The choice of ready-made blinds is now very wide and choice will depend on look, function, size, suitability, and cost.

measuring and fixing blinds

size and fittings

Ready-made shades and blinds are available in a range of sizes and can be fitted inside window recesses or on the outside, depending on the style of window, method of securing, and the look you want. Try to accommodate the standard sizes by using a larger size on a window where an overlap will not matter, or hanging a slightly smaller size inside a recess with a gap at each side. If the window is wide, consider using a number of narrow blinds in order to get the correct width, lessen the weight, and add interest. Many stores offer a made-to-measure service, but accurate measurements are crucial—luckily, most stores will do the measuring for you.

Blinds are usually sold complete with fixings and fitting instructions. Venetian blinds and roll-down shades are hung from brackets which can be screwed into the window frame, wall, ceiling, or top of the window recess. If you do not want to, or cannot, screw into the window frame, fix a support board flush with the edge of the frame and screw the fixings into that. A lot of strain is put on brackets, so make sure screws are tightly secured.

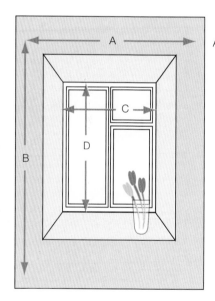

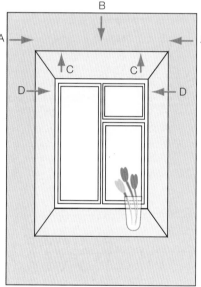

sizing up

Blinds can hang in front of the window or inside a window recess. When hanging in front, the blind should be wider than the window trim. (A). As long as the blind covers the bottom of the window, the length of the "drop" (B) need not be exact as it can be adjusted by cord or chain. To fit inside a window recess, getting a blind near the exact width (C) is crucial but the drop (D) can be adjusted.

fixing up

Blinds fitted to the outside of a window frame are usually screwed to the wall (A), but can also be screwed to the ceiling (B) if space is limited. Inside a recess, blinds can be fitted either above (C) or along the top of the window frame (D). They can also be screwed either to the top or sides of the recess, either flush against the window or at any point within the depth of the recess.

types of blind

roll-down shades

Attached to a wooden or metal rod and
pulled up and down by means of a cord.
A wooden strip slotted through the bottom
of the shade adds weight and rigidity. Kits
are available for making your own.
Plus points: discreet, lightweight.

Venetian blinds

Horizontal slats held together by cord or
tape suspended from a "box." The blind can
be pulled up and down and the slats can be
opened and closed. Available ready-made
and made-to-measure.
Plus points: control and filter the light, screen
a view, and provide privacy.

vertical blinds

Good for wide, floor-length windows. The
individual "vanes" are hung from a track
screwed to the ceiling, or wall above the
window, and are linked at the bottom.
Plus points: a long drop, easier to open and
close than horizontal blinds.

Roman blinds

Combine the uncluttered look of a blind with
the softness of curtains. Available ready-
made and made-to-measure.
Plus points: choice of a huge variety of
fabrics, easy to sew, easy to put up.

other materials

Bamboo, reed, fiber, and paper shades are
lightweight and offer a quick and simple way
of providing privacy, filtering the light or
creating a mood.
Plus points: cheap and easy to put up.

Roman blind

Roman blinds are versatile and not too difficult to make. They look crisp and modern in plain white cotton, romantic in soft, translucent muslin, or rich and luxurious in velvet. Lightweight blinds need only a cord, but for heavier fabrics and a more structured look, thin wooden slats are inserted into sewn pockets.

Roman blinds are attached to a support board screwed on above the window. To make sure you have the right measurements for the blind, mark where the board will be placed above the window before you cut your fabric. If the blind is to fit inside a window recess the dimensions of the recess will dictate the width of the board. If it is to hang in front of the window frame, allow for an overlap so the sides of the frame are covered when the blind is down.

Work out the finished size of the blind—the length will depend on its position and your personal preference. If you are using several colors, as here, sew the pieces of material together first. The width must allow for turning in along the sides.

The length comprises the length of the finished blind plus: an allowance for a hem at the bottom which is deep enough to hold a wooden slat; an allowance for a hem at the top on which you can sew a length of touch-and-close tape; the depth of the slat pockets times two (the average number of slats

is four, which means you will need to add the depth of eight pockets).

Cut a similar-size piece of lining fabric and sew onto the panel, turning in the sides, the top, and the bottom but leaving the bottom corners unstiched so that a slat can be slotted in.

Divide the panel into sections from the bottom so that the slats will be placed at regular intervals up the blind, leaving a slightly smaller space between the top slat and the support board. Mark lines at these positions across the fabric with tailors chalk. Using each line as the center of the fold, sew across the width of the blind to form a pocket wide enough to hold the wooden slat.

Press the blind and sew the touch-and-close tape along the top. Sew rings on each side of the blind at the top of each pocket. Attach screw eyelets to the underside of the support board to line up with the rings on the blind, plus one more to hold the pull cord. Tie one end of the cord to one of the bottom rings and thread it up through the other rings and the eyelets and back down to tie it to the other bottom ring, leaving enough cord at the top to pull the blind up and down.

The finished blind will look neater if you cover the board that will be fixed to the wall with matching fabric before screwing in place. Staple a length of touch-and-close tape along the front of the board to attach the blind.

step 1 Divide the panel into sections and mark the center lines of the folds, which will form the pockets for the slats.

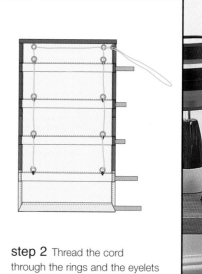

step 2 Thread the cord through the rings and the eyelets on the support board and insert the slats.

step 3 Cover a support board with fabric and staple a length of touch-and-close tape to the front. Screw in place above the window.

minimum exposure

picture window
Use your creative talents and signwriter's paint or specialist glass paints to turn a window into a work of art.

film review
Create the chic architectural look of etched glass using adhesive window film applied to clear windows.

frosty looks
There are several products which can be sprayed or painted onto windows to produce a frosty glass effect. Leave clear areas to highlight a view while maintaining privacy where windows are overlooked.

bare all
If you have beautiful windows and either you are something of an exhibitionist or you are not overlooked, eschew drapes or blinds in favor of the naked look.

under cover

mdf
Get plain MDF (medium-density fiberboard) panels cut to size at a home improvement store. Fix them using shiny stainless steel hinges for a modern look and paint them white or the same color as the wall.

off-the-rack
Ready-made doors for kitchen cabinets and closets come in a range of sizes and can be used as shutters. Louvered doors are good, as they come in narrow sizes and are quite light.

fabric
Make lightweight shutters by stretching fabric onto a frame or threading panels onto rods. Use screw hooks and eyes to fix them.

serendipity
Be adventurous and use "found" items for shutters, such as planks of weathered wood or the doors from an old cabinet.

services with a smile

the basics on electricity and water supplies

The services supplied direct to our homes—water, electricity, and, sometimes, gas—provide us with the necessities of life as well as the convenience and comfort of hot water, light, and heating. Our homes contain complex networks of water pipes and electrical wiring that are mostly hidden so that our only contact with them is at the outlet or the faucet. Connecting the supplies of water and electricity to your home is the responsibility of the relevant utility suppliers. Likewise the installation and maintenance of hot water systems and furnaces are subject to strict regulations. Any major work should always be carried out by a registered installer—failure to do so could affect any insurance claim should an accident occur. Never touch anything involving a gas supply connection; the consequences of getting it wrong can be catastrophic. Always employ a registered professional.

Keeping water in its place with good pipework and well-sealed joints is a job for a qualified plumber but, in the event of a leak, knowing where the shutoff valve is can avert disaster while waiting for him to arrive.

We take electricity for granted and are mostly aware of its dangers, but sometimes, unknowingly, we take risks by overloading an outlet or using the wrong light bulb.

Understanding the relationship between watts, volts, and amps will help avoid potential hazards.

Minor incidents such as a dripping faucet or a blown fuse are irritating but not life threatening and can be easily remedied. However, they can also be an indication of something wrong with the system or a worse problem elsewhere. If fuses or light bulbs are frequently having to be replaced, it could be due to a fault in the electrical wiring, and if the sound of a dripping faucet doesn't drive you mad, the realization that the drips have seeped through a poor seal and formed a large puddle elsewhere can make you very cross indeed.

It makes sense to be cautious when dealing with water and electricity, so confine your home improvement enthusiasms to the outside of faucets, outlets, and light fixtures, leaving the complexities of water systems and electrical circuits to the appropriate expert plumber or electrician. However, there are many opportunities to improve your environment using some of the huge range of plug-in lighting and appliances, and it may be that the disappointing flow from your shower does not need an expensive plumbing job to rectify it but simply is a matter of screwing on a new showerhead.

problems with your waterworks

Though not as inherently dangerous as gas or electricity, even a small amount of water in the wrong place can cause a huge amount of damage. A steady drip, undetected over a period of time, can cause as much damage as a full-scale flood, so it pays to be alert and make sure that everything is sealed and watertight.

flooding

In case of a sudden and dramatic leakage, turn off the main shutoff valve immediately. If the source of the leak is not immediately apparent (check that a hose hasn't become disconnected), call a plumber.

shutoff valves

A shutoff valve on the main water supply line enables you to turn off the water supply in case of an emergency, or to carry out work on the system. It is important to know where this is. In most homes it is found where the supply enters your home, but the location varies. There will be additional shutoff valves so that the water supply can be disconnected to individual items— such as sinks, showers, toilets, refrigerators.

leaks

Small leaks can cause enormous damage to a home, especially if undetected for any length of time. Drips, damp, or funny smells can indicate a leak so always investigate.

damaged pipes

Cracks occur in pipes for a variety of reasons including age, puncturing with a nail or freezing. Hairline cracks are difficult to detect and as the leaked water often travels along the outside of the pipe before dripping off, the location of the wet patch does not always coincide with the leak.

If accessible, repair the pipe temporarily by binding it with the very sticky strong plumbing tape specifically made for the job. Hairline cracks can turn into large fissures, so get the pipe replaced by a plumber.

bad seals

Water can get through extremely small gaps; silicone caulk around bathtubs and sinks are particularly vulnerable. Remove all traces of old caulk using a special solvent and replace, making sure that all surfaces are perfectly dry when applying.

Top tip: when sealing around a tub, fill it with water and leave until the caulk has set. If you don't, the weight of water and the bather will pull the caulk away from the wall and break the seal.

leaking joints

Joints and seals on pipework, waste pipes, and connections to appliances are common sources of leaks. Areas behind bathtub panels, sinks, washing machines, and dishwashers are particularly vulnerable, so take a look from time to time.

Common causes are loose connections, worn threads, and worn washers. Try tightening everything up using a wrench if necessary (but don't force anything).

If water still escapes wind tephlon tape (a very thin plastic tape available from home improvement and plumbing stores) around the thread and retighten. Replace any washers and if the problem still persists, replace the whole joint.

Hose connectors and plastic drain trapes are easy to repair yourself, but it is advisable to employ a plumber for metal pipework.

fixing a dripping faucet

The most common reason for a faucet to drip is a worn washer. Changing a washer is another classic of the do-it-yourself world and therefore no self-respecting, handywoman likes to admit to calling in a plumber for such an apparently simple task. There are, however, many different styles and designs of faucets. Some don't have washers and others are very difficult to get into—so don't feel a wimp if you do resort to using a plumber.

Modern faucets may have ceramic discs or rubber O rings in place of washers. Ceramic discs are supposed to be maintenance free so should not need replacing. As the ceramic disc is incorporated into a cartridge, just order a new one of the correct size for that specific tap. O rings can be relatively easy to replace. Examining the inside of your faucets will determine whether it is possible to carry out maintenance yourself—but remember to always turn off the shutoff valve before unscrewing a faucet!

If you have an old-fashioned faucet (as illustrated) then changing a washer is not complicated. You may need to take the old washer to the home improvement store to find the right replacement, so don't decide to do it when the stores are closed. If you are daunted by the inside workings and can't work out what is what, seek the advice of a plumber who may recommend a new faucet (which won't necessarily cost a fortune) if yours is old or of poor quality.

turn it off!

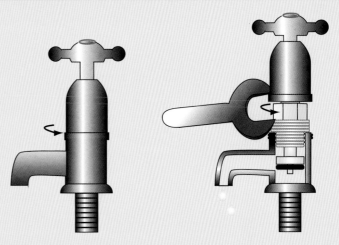

Turn off the water at the shutoff valve. Unscrew the cover and lift to reveal the "head-gear" nut and unscrew it using a wrench.

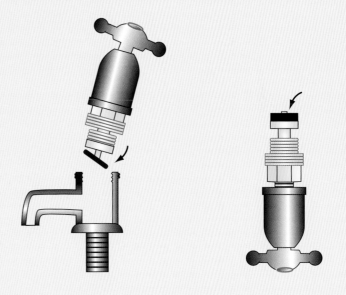

Lift out the top section of the faucet, remove the old washer, and replace with a new one of the correct size.

going with the flow

Don't let unpleasant blockages interfere with the flow!

main attraction

Most homes are connected to the main water supply line which enters the home through the main shutoff valve. Water is then distributed around the home via a system of a pipes to feed tanks, faucets, and appliances such as washing machines and dishwashers.

waste management

All waste water is channeled to the sewer line through drain lines. Bathtubs, showers, sinks, and washing machines drain eventually into a single pipe connected to the sewer drainage, but the toilet is connected to a separate drain pipe. The drains are vented upward through vents higher up. These let in air and allow water to flow freely.

quenching that thirst

Water from faucets directly connected to the main water line is suitable for drinking. Some foreign countries have indirect stored water systems. In these systems only some faucets are connected directly to the main water supply and the others are fed from cold-water storage tanks. It is not advisable to drink water from storage tanks as it is not fresh and may contain impurities picked up from the tank or surroundings.

softening up

The quality of your local water can affect your supply. In hard water areas a buildup of limescale inside pipework, around faucets, and showerheads can reduce the flow. There are several products on the market which remove or reduce the buildup of limescale. Always read the instructions as many are unsuitable for materials such as enamel.

There are several water-softening systems available and many people are choosing to put in a water-filtering system to improve the quality of drinking water. For advice and installation always use a reputable supplier.

Showers are particularly vulnerable to limescale and lack of water pressure both of which may improve by replacing the showerhead and the hose both of which are usually fixed with a simple screw fitting. A wide variety are available at home improvement and plumbing stores.

unblocking sinks and toilets

Drain lines leading from sinks, toilets, and showers have a bend or trap where a small amount of trapped water prevents sewage odors entering the home. These traps are perfect places for blockages. Sinks are usually fitted with a plastic trap with an access cap which can be unscrewed allowing blockages to be cleared. There may also be an access cap on the branch pipe (a straight run of pipe beyond the trap) and this can be cleared using a hooked wire.

However, there are lots of blockage-clearing products for putting down drains and toilet bowls that will fizz and foam to break down waste substances that have built up. Sometimes it takes more than one application.

Caustic soda is a highly efficient shifter of blockages but should be used with care. It is available over the counter

as a powder which, when mixed with water, becomes alarmingly hot and steamy. Follow very carefully the instructions on the packaging, wear thick rubber gloves, and don't inhale the fumes. All these products are potentially corrosive so keep them away from surfaces, clothes, and skin.

If the problem persists, this may indicate a more serious blockage farther down the drain line—if you're unsure, call in that plumber!

fixing tanks and float balls

If the toilet tank isn't filling take the lid off (providing it is accessible) to inspect the mechanisms inside. Make sure that the float ball arm is not stuck in the up position.

If the tank is continuously filling check that the valve is working. If water is pouring out through the overflow check that the float is adjusted so that the level of water is below the overflow outlet. A toilet will run because water is leaking in or leaking out. The adjustment needed for water leaking in is with the ballcock or float. For water leaking out, check the lift chain or wire,

or the tank ball or flapper. Whether you deal with these problems yourself will depend on whether any replacement parts are simple to obtain and replace. Your home improvement store might be able to help.

live wires

Electricity is potentially dangerous if not treated with respect and caution. We tend to take it for granted, only noticing it when something doesn't work or we have run out of outlets for our ever-expanding collection of electrical appliances.

Electricity is distributed around our homes along cables and wires which feed the electricity to outlets and light fixtures. Amateurs are advised to leave any work involving the actual supply to professional electricians. However, awareness of the principles of electricity supply will help you use it responsibly and make you see the wisdom of leaving certain jobs to qualified electricians who know about these things.

short circuits

Electricity is supplied to individual homes through a cable to a distribution box (service panel). From here power is distributed to all the separate circuits supplying lighting, outlets, and individual appliances such as kitchen ranges.

Each circuit is connected to a circuit breaker which carries a fuse that blows if there is a fault such as overloading or a loose wire. Modern circuit breakers are incorporated into a switch which is thrown when the fuse blows making it easy to identify which circuit has the problem as the switch will be in the "off" position. When the problem has been identified and dealt with the switch can be switched back to the "on" position.

Older types of fuse carriers have a fuse wire (which breaks and needs replacing before the power can be restored to the circuit) or a fuse cartridge. Replacing them is a simple operation but it is imperative that the fuse rating corresponds to the circuit and the correct fuse or gauge of wire is used. If you use a high rating fuse or wire on a low rating circuit the circuit would not know it was overloaded and the fuse wouldn't blow. Fuses are rated in amps: lighting circuits usually use 5-15 amp fuses, ring circuits use 20- or 30-amp fuses, and certain appliances such as kitchen ranges may need a 40-45 amp fuse. A main switch on the service panel allows the electricity supply to be shut off while fuses are being replaced.

current conductor

Electricity is conducted along cables and wires through a medium which is usually copper wire. The earth beneath our feet is also a very efficient conductor of electricity and any that escapes through exposed or unconnected wires will flow toward the ground, taking the shortest route and passing through any object in its way. If you happen to be touching that object, or are the object itself, the consequences range from a mild buzzing sensation to instant death.

It is for this reason a grounding wire is included in wiring systems to channel wayward electric current to the earth via the incoming electricity supply cable. A ground fault will not necessarily cause the circuit to cut out and therefore it is still possible to get an electric shock, but ground leakage protection will break the circuit when any leakage passes through an outside conductor (which could be a person).

Ground leakage protection can be included in the distribution box so the whole electricity supply throughout the home is protected. Otherwise it can be provided for individual appliances by using ground-fault circuit-interupter (GFCI) wall outlets.

Metal water pipes, bathtubs, and radiators are all potential conductors of electricity and are connected to a separate grounding wire that leads directly to the service panel and this should always be carried out by a qualified electrician.

There are codes governing electrical wiring and these vary from region to region. Always get a qualified electrician to carry out any work on outlets indoors near water (bathrooms or kitchens) or outdoors, if you are unsure about local codes. Remember that water is a good conductor of electricity. Don't operate switches with wet hands and keep all appliances a safe distance from the water source. Never use an extension cable in a bathroom to plug in appliances such as heaters.

Warning! Do not switch circuits back on or replace fuses until the problem has been identified and dealt with. If in doubt as to what the fault is, consult an electrician.

what's watt?

Computer equipment, stereo systems, radios, and lamps require less power than appliances that produce heat.

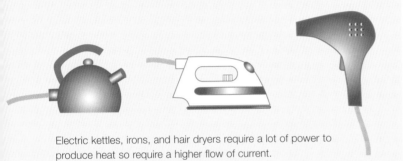

Electric kettles, irons, and hair dryers require a lot of power to produce heat so require a higher flow of current.

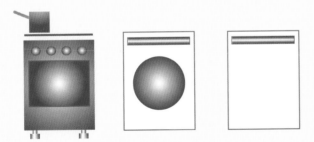

Kitchen ranges should always be connected to their own dedicated circuit. Washing machines and refrigerators can usually be plugged into an ordinary outlet.

Two simple sums enable you to work out the power needed to operate an appliance.

Watts ÷ Volts = Amps (type of cord required)
Amps x Volts = Watts (power required to run appliance)

Trying to understand amps, volts, and watts can tie your brain in knots, but it is pretty obvious that a dryer requires more power (watts) and therefore a higher flow of current (amps) than a light bulb. It also follows that a dryer needs to run from a higher powered circuit than lighting so the plug on a washing machine needs a higher amp fuse than the plug on a desk lamp.

Most outlet circuits are at least 15 amps and, as the average washing machine needs 3.0 kW (3,000 watts) of power, you can work out using the calculations that one outlet will run one washing machine. A table lamp with a 60-watt light bulb will require less than 4 amps and so using an adaptor and running two lamps off the same outlet will be okay.

Power-hungry items such as ranges and water heaters are given their own circuits with their own circuit breaker to cope with their high demand for energy. Information on wattage and amperage will be marked or printed on a label somewhere on the appliance and in the instructions, but it is not always easy to understand especially as they may also include different specifications relating to other countries in which the item is also sold.

Amateurs should not attempt any work on circuits, switches, or outlets. Any dealings with electricity should be kept to outside an outlet, leaving anything on the other side to a qualified electrician.

switched on

plugged in

Know your plugs and prevent crossed wires and possible disasters.

wiring a plug

All new appliances now come ready supplied with a fused plug but knowing how to wire a plug is necessary for dealing with loose wires.

Some plugs have three terminals—one each for the grounding, neutral, and live connections. The positioning of each is usually indicated.

To wire a plug, strip the plastic casing off the end of the wires using wire strippers or a sharp blade so the connector is in direct contact with the terminal. Bend over the ends to make them neat and solid and connect to the terminal. On clamp terminals the wire is wrapped around a threaded post and secured by a screw nut while on a post terminal the wire is poked into a hole and held in position by a screw. Check that the conductor is held securely.

Although a grounded three-pin plug is the standard in the U.S., if you are on vacation in Europe, you will notice that continental Europe use two-pin ungrounded plugs. In the United Kingdom, however, the three-pin plug is the norm. These plugs have fuses built into them. The fuses are used as a circuit-breaking precaution and the correct amp fuse must be used for each appliance.

Double insulated appliances must not be grounded and therefore the cord will be a twin sheathed type. It is still okay to use a standard plug and leave the grounding terminal unconnected.

sorting out outlets

The number of appliances we plug into our electricity supply has increased enormously in recent years and few old homes have enough outlets to take them all. In order to avoid dangerously overloaded outlets it is both safer and more convenient to use trailing outlets which have a row of two or more outlets and plug into a wall outlet.

Trailing outlets are ideal for items such as computers, printers, and lamps which are relatively low wattage. Such outlets, however, should not be abused—it is better to get an electrician to put in extra outlets than risk overloading the circuit.

Power surges can occur in our electricity supply, sometimes from faults on our own circuits but also occasionally in the supply from the electricity provider. Computers and other sensitive electronic equipment can be sensitive to such surges and so it is a good idea to use plugs or trailing outlets (or get an electrician to fit a special outlet) fitted with a "surge supressor."

The standard U.K. three-pin plug (left) is grounded using earth (green and yellow), neutral (blue), and live (brown) wires. A twin-sheathed cord is also used (right) that requires no grounding connection.

The standard U.S. three-pin plug (left) is grounded using earth (green), neutral (white), and live (black) wires. The U.S. round cord plug (right) has no grounding connection, only neutral and live wires.

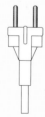

The two-pin ungrounded plug is commonly used throughout continental Europe and is a sealed unit attached to the appliance. Other shapes and sizes are occasionally used.

Computer and entertainment equipment gets more stylish all the time so need not detract from a stylish interior. Unless electric cords and cable cords are kept under control they can look unsightly. How you deal with them can vary from hiding them away altogether, feeding them through specially designed cord covers, or turning them into a feature.

Whatever you do, keep cables organized—labeled, if necessary, and accessible. Keep all wiring safe from accidental disconnection by feet, children, and pets. The simplest way is to gather the wires together and tie them with plastic wire ties, string, or even fancy ribbon. Screw hooks under a desk or table and loop them up out of sight and out of danger.

Flexible plastic sleeving is available through which several cables can be fed for a neat, businesslike look. Alternatively, fix panels to walls, table backs, or desk legs to hide all cables and plugs. Place TVs and sound systems on lidded boxes or chests. Drill holes so any cables can be fed through and kept inside. Drill holes in shelves or use bracketed shelving systems with gaps at the back.

bright ideas

well hidden

Add light above a worktop or in an alcove using small low-voltage lights concealed behind a fascia. Use a kit—a set of lights each with its own connection that plugs into a transformer—that plugs into a wall outlet. Look for short strip lights with a plug attached.

well washed

Use similar kits to produce washes of light up or down walls. Put them behind a fascia (made from a length of wood screwed to support boards) in an alcove or across the whole wall at ceiling height or eye level. Direct the light up or down or let it shine from behind or down edges.

Christmas all year round

Drape strings of small Christmas lights above a bed or along a shelf for a gentle, twinkly effect.

surprise lights

Tiny bulbs set into flexible tubing can bring light to unexpected places—behind the couch or in a bowl on a table. Hang them on the wall and turn them into works of art bending them into simple spirals.

bare necessity

For the pared-down modern look, throw away the lampshade and use naked bulbs making the most of the wide range of shapes and sizes from large globes to tiny candles.

leading light

Careful or adventurous use of light can alter or enhance the ambience of an interior.

lighting the way

Putting in new light fixtures can be fairly straightforward in terms of wiring. Other considerations, however, such as making holes in ceilings or walls, securing light fixtures, and working out the load on the circuit, make it a more complicated job best left to a qualified electrician.

There is now a wide range of different types of lighting that plugs into a wall outlet, so is much easier to install than connecting into the lighting circuit. As well as table lamps and work lights, there are various spots, downlighters, strip lights, and ropelights which can add mood and style as well as extra light.

watts and voltage

Some lights and lighting systems are low voltage (operating at 12 or 24 volts) and need a transformer to reduce the domestic supply from main-supply voltage to the required lower voltage.

With reputable brands and high-quality equipment the transformer is usually included with the fixture, either incorporated into the lamp itself, the plug, a separate plug-in section on the cord, or even into the bulb. If a separate transformer is needed, then specifications and instructions on connection will be included. There are strict rules governing all lighting sold to ensure that it conforms to the requirements of safety standards as well as the electricity supply, so if you are tempted to buy inexpensive lights, or have bought something in another country, either make sure that they conform to these regulations, or don't buy them.

Many downlighter and track systems operate with low voltage lights, so even though you are not installing it yourself, impress (and annoy) your electrician by checking that a transformer is incorporated into the system.

The world of light bulbs is complex and it is important not to exceed the recommended wattage as you could be overloading the circuit—take particular care with tracks or rows of spotlights and sets of downlighters. Information on maximum recommended wattage is printed on, or included in the instructions for most domestic lighting and now that there are low voltage lamps on the market it is important to take note of the voltage, bearing in mind that low voltage bulbs can only be used with light fixtures that have, or are connected to a transformer. Using a higher watt bulb in a fitting can cause damage from overheating.

light bulbs

Traditional tungsten light bulbs have bases with a screw thread (right). Some European bulbs have two side pins that fit into special sockets (left).

Reflector spotlight bulbs are used for downlighters and spotlights. Tungsten bulbs are also available in a variety of shapes and sizes.

The compact fluorescent bulb (left) gives a bright light and is energy efficient. Halogen reflector light bulbs (right) are frequently used in downlighting systems as well as desk lamps.

domestic bliss

cleaning and caring for your home

A sure sign of being grown-up is a willingness to clean your bedroom without being issued with an ultimatum. Cleaning has become sexy and huge numbers of born-again cleaners are coming out of their well-ordered closets to proclaim the pleasures of household maintenance.

The therapeutic benefits of home maintenance include the cathartic effects of cleaning out a closet and the calming effects of a fashionably uncluttered environment. Venting your anger on the floor rather than a loved one can leave you, and the floor, feeling remarkably refreshed. Cleaning is a way of restoring order into your life as well as your home. Taking pleasure in simple daily tasks is very Zen, but it does put you in touch with possessions and surroundings reminding you how nice (or horrible) they are, and making you aware of the benefits of keeping them in good order (or throwing them out).

We know and appreciate the benefits of clean clothes yet often fail to impose similar standards of care and cleanliness on our environment. However, now that the style of our homes has become as important as what we wear, freshly laundered linens and a nicely ironed cushion cover can make us feel just as confident as a well-pressed suit and brand new underwear. Apart from the obvious aesthetic advantages of a well-kept house, the practical aspects are many. Not only will things look better if they are cleaned regularly, they will also last longer. Caring for your house will not only save you money on maintenance and repairs but will help retain its value and make it easier to sell or rent.

We are all more health-conscious nowadays and aware of the hazards of dust and pollutants in the atmosphere. Regular cleaning and good ventilation can often control and prevent allergies, and remember—it's not always food that gives us food poisoning; it can be the dishcloth!

A clean, tidy room is more conducive to relaxation, and if you value your home and appreciate the joys of interior decoration, you will probably also enjoy cleaning. Even if you don't, you may be able to turn it into a pleasurable activity by investing in a few gadgets and some of the many wonderful (and sometimes weird) products and potions available to make things easier, quicker, and more fun. Our homes speak volumes about our personalities, so if you want yours to say something nice, it makes sense to look after it.

10 essential cleaning tools

Those already tuned-in to the pleasures of housework will cheerfully change their mops and dusters as often as their clothes, but even those who still consider cleaning a chore will find it hard to resist some of the new fashionable designs and colors now available in homeware departments.

broom

For sweeping up the fascinating collection of fluff, grit, dust, and crumbs that are part of any normal interior. Soft bristles will gather the dust as well as the bits and will poke more easily into corners.

dustpan and brush

Essential not only for the collection and disposal of sweepings but also a safe way to gather up broken glass or china and minor disasters, such as spilt cereal boxes.

mop

You can get down on your hands and knees to clean a floor but using a mop and bucket is easier. For wet work, the mops made from strips of cloth are best. A soft mop, used dry, is good for dusting floors.

bucket

Everyone needs a bucket at some time. Plastic is cheap and cheerful, but chic. Galvanized metal, stainless steel, and white enamel are very designer but also heavy and noisy.

cloths and dusters

Whether you invest in the latest hi-tech duster or just use an old rag, a plentiful selection of cleaning cloths is as essential as a good supply of underwear. Use cotton dishcloths, fluffy dusters, and linen scrim.

scrubbing brushes

There comes a time when a good old-fashioned scrub is the only way to get things clean. Choose from bristly, country wooden ones to the chic, modern cool plastics.

scourers

Flat, nylon scourers (available on their own or stuck to a sponge) are good for cleaning pans, but are also great for scrubbing off built-up dirt and deposits. They are perfect for washing paintwork in preparation for painting or just giving furniture or flower pots a good clean.

toothbrushes

There must be a hundred and one uses for an old toothbrush. Cleaning around the bases of faucets, the corners of window frames, and the crevices of ornaments are just three of them.

vacuum cleaner

A vacuum cleaner is the domestic equivalent of a best friend. Vacuuming is the only really efficient way of removing dust and can be used for everything from floors to furniture.

sponges

Available in lots of shapes, sizes, and compositions. Big foam sponges are fine for sloshing on lots of suds but not so good at mopping them up. More expensive, heavier ones are more absorbent and more efficient, while small, natural sponges used for make-up are great for cleaning delicate objects.

10 essential cleaning products

Bring a sparkle to your life with a few basic cleaning products.

spit and polish

The joys of housework are not obvious to everyone, but few would deny the pleasures of a freshly cleaned room. Fussy fanatics may extol the virtues of daily dusting and vigorous vacuuming but hectic lives often dictate that precious time is spent waxing legs rather than floors. However, unless you are a complete slob, basic chores such as cleaning sinks and bathtubs will need doing, but there is no mystique, and no need for a closet full of cleaning potions and lotions. A good vacuum cleaner, a plentiful supply of clean cloths, and a few basic cleaning materials are all that is required. And once you have accepted that pristine perfection only exists in magazine interiors, the dreaded housework will seem less daunting and, who knows, even a delight.

There are vast numbers of cleaning products suitable for all sorts of cleaning tasks and problems, many of which you didn't realize you had! The good news is that while some of them are undoubtedly very efficient (and expensive) you can keep a perfectly clean house with just a few basics. Cleansers contain varying combinations of detergent (used to dissolve grease and dirt), abrasives (to cut through more stubborn layers), and disinfectant (to kill germs and sterilize). Overzealous cleaning with strong, powerful cleansers can seriously damage your home so choose all-purpose cleaners, which are usually mild and, unless stated on the label, will be suitable for most surfaces.

cream cleanser

Slightly abrasive but not harsh enough to damage smooth surfaces. Use on sinks, bathtubs, toilets, and very grubby or stained countertops. Squeeze directly onto the surface and rub with a wet sponge, plastic scourer, or cloth.

general-purpose floor and surface cleaner

Available in liquid form. Dissolve in warm water for mopping floors and washing countertops, kitchen surfaces, and paintwork, or use neat for deeper dirt. It is nonabrasive and so ideal for wiping off cookers and appliances. Contains detergent which will dissolve grease as well as dirt.

window and glass cleaner

There are many theories on the best way to clean windows but a proprietary spray cleaner is the easiest. Several contain vinegar which adds to the cleaning power. Spray on and rub off with a soft cloth.

bleach

Chlorine-based liquid which kills germs and bleaches. Used for drain holes, sinks, and toilets and for sterilizing countertops, equipment, etc. Use a weak solution for washing or soaking and a stronger solution, or neat, for bleaching out stains.

mild soap and detergent

Useful for a good scrub or a gentle wash. Contain no harsh ingredients so are suitable for more delicate surfaces and as a frequent-wash cleaner. You can still get blocks of household soap which is mild and relatively free from added chemicals. Eco-friendly brands of dishwashing liquid are also good and easier to use.

white vinegar

Good for removing scum and soap buildup from bathtubs and showers. Use diluted in water to clean windows and mirrors. Will neutralize odors including pet accidents. Use with baking soda to make foaming homemade cleaners. It is acidic so don't use on porous surfaces such as grouting.

baking soda

Has abrasive and deodorizing properties and is brilliant at removing stains. Can be used on clothes, carpets, and wallpaper as well as stained teapots, vacuum flasks, and casserole dishes. Dissolves grease and mineral deposits and makes a powerful cleanser for sinks when mixed with vinegar.

soda water

Keep a bottle handy for emergency action for spills on clothes and carpeting. The fizz brings the stain to the surface so it can be blotted up.

lemon juice

A natural bleach and disinfectant. Use instead of bleach to remove stains on clothes, countertops, and hands. However, use with caution and never allow it to come into contact with any form of stone as it literally burns the material and resulting stains and marks cannot be removed.

borax

A general-purpose cleaner that has been used for centuries. It is an important ingredient in alternative homemade cleansers. Not as corrosive as vinegar or lemon juice.

basic home care

Keep up appearances with the following surface treatments.

floors

Walking on floors causes damage—our feet efficiently grind in the dirt, grit, and grime of everday life and gradually wear away the surface, so regular removal of these substances will keep floors looking good and prolong their life.

A vaccum cleaner is the most effective way of removing dust and can be used on all floors (but don't use the beating type of vacuum cleaner on hard or shiny floors as it will scratch). Use the attachments to suck up dust around edges and underneath things. Few people have the time (or the inclination) to vacuum every day so keep a broom, dusting mop, or carpet sweeper handy for the big bits such as crumbs, spills, and things brought in on the soles of shoes.

Dirt and grease can be removed from vinyl, concrete, and ceramic floors with a proprietry floor cleaner (but for stone floors use soap). To prevent smears on very shiny tiles, dry with an old towel or absorbent cloth. Unglazed tiles such as quarry tiles will absorb more dirt and may need an occasional good scrub using a slightly abrasive cleaner—don't use soap as it will leave a dull film.

The grout between the tiles can become dirty and stained—scrub periodically with detergent or an abrasive cleaner using a brush. Remove scuff marks and grease with a small amount of neat cleaner or mineral spirits on a cloth.

When mopping use a double bucket or two buckets, one with detergent or cleaner and the other with clean water. Rinse the mop in clean water after each wipe, otherwise you are redistributing the dirt around the floor rather than cleaning it. Don't slosh water around and leave the surface as dry as possible by giving the mop a good squeeze.

Don't use water on wooden floors, although polyurethane varnish or laminated floor finishes can be mopped or washed using warm water with a few drops of mild detergent and a very well-squeezed out cloth or mop. For waxed or oiled floors, which are very beautiful and (usually) very precious, vacuum or dust frequently using a dusting mop and only rewax if the floor is dull or very dirty.

There are several products that offer protection, stain resistance, instant shine, and several other tempting easy-care opportunities. Use these with caution as they often build up over time into a coating that becomes dull, dirty, and worn and takes a lot of effort to remove. Some floors may need sealing or resealing and old dirty floors can be rejuvenated using a range of special treatments and products. Always ask advice from a specialist—manufacturers often have a helpline and you could find yourself engaged in conversation with an enthusiastic, knowledgeable boffin who will recommend the correct product and treatment.

countertops

Countertops should be washed or wiped frequently using a clean cloth. A solution of bleach will kill germs. Wooden countertops need occassional re-oiling, but you can dab sunflower oil on dry patches in between oilings. Never allow lemon juice to come into contact with stone—it burns into the surface.

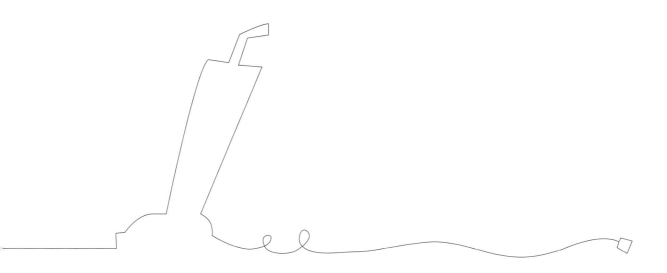

tiles

Wall tiles can be washed with almost any proprietry cleaner, but a buildup of grease in kitchens and soap scum in bathrooms may require more effort.

Wiping tiles daily after cooking or each shower or bath will prevent grease, soap, and water deposits from forming, but this requires discipline (and can quite spoil the effects of a relaxing bath). For once it is a good idea to invest in a special tile and grout cleaner and give your tiles a good clean only when you feel the need.

windows and walls

Use a spray window-cleaner for glass and rub off with clean, lint-free cloths. If windows are very dirty wash them with warm water and detergent first, dry thoroughly, and then if they lack sparkle, follow up with spray cleaner.

You can remove marks from painted walls using a mild detergent and a sponge or cloth; however, this tends to remove the paint and leave a discolored patch. Repainting the whole wall is often easier.

bathrooms

Even if you hate all housework you will want to keep sinks, bathtubs, showers, and toilets looking, and smelling, sweet. Don't go mad on the bleaches and disinfectants; it is much better for you, and the environment, to clean regularly. However, hard water causes limescale buildup so be prepared to resort to fizzy tablets in the toilet and limescale remover for faucets.

furniture

Furniture responds well to regular dusting, vacuuming, and a bit of buffing up. A duster slightly dampened with a little water or spray cleaner will pick up dust efficiently and freshen up plastic and metal. Give wood an occasional polish with a good-quality wax polish. A vacuum cleaner with a good set of tools is best for upholstery—the brush attachment is brilliant for drapes and shades.

electrical equipment

Electrical equipment, such as computers and TVs, attract dust via static electricity. Remove the dust frequently with a vacuum cleaner—the brush attachment can be used on keyboards—and you can also use a duster dampened with an antistatic cleaner. It is probably better not to use liquids around electrical items, so it is worth investing in computer screen-cleaning wipes and specialist equipment cleaner.

10 handy housework hints

Whether you are a fanatical, furniture-polishing fusspot or cheerfully slovenly, a few tips are always welcome to help get rid of the grubby patches, greasy splodges, and nasty things that lurk in corners and are a product of normal life.

glove love
Use protection, dress for the part, and greet all your cleaning tasks with utmost enthusiasm. Gloves—rubber for wet work, fleecy lined for dusting—are essential for protecting those hands and nails. Buy yourself a special cleaning outfit—perhaps a huge printed shirt and a pair of brightly colored jogging pants.

shower power
Clean grubby plastic or metal-slatted blinds in the shower or bathtub using the shower attachment, a soft brush, and mild detergent.

tidy tools
Keep cleaning materials accessible in a nice box or basket to complement the decor—it will encourage you to use them more often.

scented dusters
Sprinkle a few drops of lavender oil on a duster and spread perfume as you go.

shopping trips
Visit the cleaning department of a big store and be tempted by the array of crisp, checked cloths, deliciously soft dusters, prettily patterned gloves, and brilliant gadgets and products.

tapping in
For clean, shiny faucets use tooth paste (the cream type—gel won't work). Rub it on with your fingers and rinse well.

eco deco
Go eco-friendly and make your own nonscratch cleanser by mixing $3/4$ cup baking soda with $1/4$ cup borax and enough washing-up liquid to form a smooth paste.

clean machine
Don't forget to keep cleaning equipment clean—wash dusters and cloths after use, wash mop heads and brooms from time to time, and empty the vacuum cleaner frequently.

sweet feet
Buy several pairs of slippers for your guests to use—your friends will think you're crazy, but who wants dirty feet on your newly cleaned floors?

fizz whizz
Clean glass vases by filling with warm water and dropping in one or two denture tablets and allow to soak overnight.

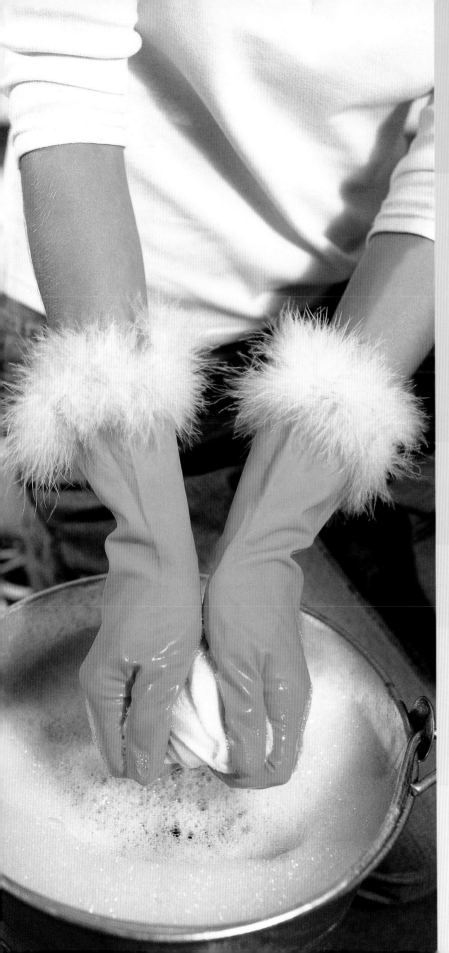

stain removal

Accidents are inevitable, but tough stains can be tackled. Most spills respond to prompt action with mild detergent, bleach, soda water, or a proprietary spot cleaner. Some products are unsuitable for certain materials, so check before using. Rust, mildew, and damp patches can be an indication of a more serious problem; find out the cause before dealing with them.

Tea, coffee, red wine, and cola can be removed with soda water. Mop up any excess, pour on soda water, and soak up with clean rags. You shouldn't have to rub, but if you do, always work from the outside in to avoid spreading the stain.

Treat discoloration with cream cleanser and bleach or various mixes of lemon juice, vinegar, and bicarbonate of soda.

Keep a proprietary spot cleaner handy for difficult stains such as ink or dye; apply immediately and then follow instructions.

Tackle stains in stainless steel or porcelain sinks with cream cleanser or, if that fails, a solution of liquid chlorine bleach.

Wash out grease with mild detergent— eco-friendly dishwashing liquid is gentle.

Wash mildew stains off walls with mild bleach solution; treat any discoloration with stain sealer before repainting.

Remove stains and marks from wallpaper by rubbing them gently with white bread.

Scented flowers and plants not only smell wonderful but can look wonderful, too. Seasonal flowers will help you keep in touch with the rhythm of nature's cycle.

A large bowl of apples can scent a whole room, especially if they are freshly picked. Gently browning bananas smell pleasantly sweet.

Keep linens smelling good with lavender oil or linen spray. Place muslin bags filled with lavender and rosemary between sheets. Add drops of lavender oil to pillows for a dreamy sleep.

Bunches of herbs hung in the kitchen will offer a subtle aroma while giving the impression that you are a keen and inspired cook.

Make your own deodorizers by sprinkling drops of vanilla or essential oils onto a cotton pad, refreshing when necessary.

Keep moths away with cedar wood and lavender rather than moth balls. Stores sell a variety of wooden shapes and sachets to hang in your closet or place between clothes in drawers.

a breath of fresh air

There are many reasons for keeping the outside world at bay—noise, pollution, and cold being the main ones. But although it is prudent to prevent expensively produced heat from escaping through badly fitting windows and doors, it is unhealthy, and even dangerous, to seal yourself in too tightly. We are familiar with the concept of "fresh air" being good for you, but we tend to associate it with spending time outdoors. In fact, the air in our homes is constantly being changed and circulated, entering and leaving via specially fitted vents and venting systems as well as chimneys, open windows and doors, and gaps around baseboards, doors, and windows. Ventilation is considered adequate when the air in our homes changes at least ten times per day—a surprising amount of air activity! Anything less than that and the buildup of pollutants in the air can be dangerous.

sick house syndrome

It is easy to get paranoid about fumes, fungi, viruses, and other VOCs (volatile organic compounds), convincing ourselves that we, and our houses, are "sick." But even if we lived in a mud hut and eschewed all "dangerous" modern materials such as paint, cleaning products, and cosmetics, the smoke of our wood fire and the straw on the roof expose us to equally harmful substances. However, by living in well-equipped, stylish homes we are probably surrounded by more noxious substances than is good for us and we tend to increase any potential danger by cutting down on natural ventilation in order to conserve energy used in heating. Once you are aware of the need for air circulation it is relatively easy to ensure that windows are open (even a small opening is sufficient) throughout the house and that all vents are unblocked. There are strict health and safety regulations regarding the installation of vents, so it is important to check that yours comply. If you are renting, get proof that this has been done from your landlord. Lack of ventilation can make us feel drowsy, head-achey, and generally unwell, so before reaching for pills or the medical dictionary try opening a window.

humidity

It is not only pollutants in the air that make good ventilation essential: lack of air circulation increases humidity and therefore the risk of mildew and damp. Bathrooms and kitchens are particularly vulnerable. Opening windows to allow steam to escape is a simple way of keeping the atmosphere relatively dry, but if mildew or condensation persists it may be necessary to install a fan or extra vent. Not only is damp and mildew unsightly, and often smelly, it can do extensive damage to the structure of a home. Air needs to be able to circulate in hidden areas, including the roof space and underneath floors, and overzealous insulation and unsuitable floorcoverings can add to the problem. If you are experiencing damp problems in upstairs rooms, get someone to check the roofspace and make sure that air is getting in and out. Before laying an impervious floorcovering such as laminated or vinyl floorings make sure that it will not prevent air circulating below the floor as this can lead to damage.

nice smells

Homes that smell nice are undoubtedly nicer to live in, but we can get carried away with inappropriate and invasive use of room fragrances. A clean, well-ventilated room shouldn't smell bad. If it does there may be a problem, e.g. damp, or something decomposing under the floorboards. We have become obsessed with smells and there are many products on the market that prey on our insecurities, offering us odor-free bathrooms and peach-scented living rooms. The perfumes in many of these products are artificially created using chemicals that only add to the pollution of the air rather than "purifying" it. It is wise to avoid aerosols, which are not eco-friendly and often contain unpleasant additives. Surrounding ourselves with heavy scents will desensitize our noses and prevent us from appreciating the subtler nuances of flowers, herbs, wood, or freshly laundered linens.

leave it to the experts

when and how to call in the professionals

Once you have experienced the thrill of doing it yourself, it is easy to get carried away and start planning other more ambitious projects. This is fine if the results of your first efforts surpassed your expectations both in ease of doing and quality of finish, and doing them revealed hitherto unsuspected talents you never dreamed you had. Graduating from putting up a shelf to installing a countertop, or from tiling a backsplash to tiling a whole bathroom may only require one or two extra skills and a little more research, time and effort, so go ahead and plan. However, it may be that you found the work less enjoyable, easy, and straightforward than you had hoped, and the finish not quite up to your high standards, in which case you are wise to limit your home improvement activities to simple necessities such as putting up the occasional coat hook and ready-made shelf. Either way, the experience and knowledge gained from doing it yourself will allow you to assess the extent or limits of your skills and so help you decide whether to take on a job or call in a professional.

Understanding the complexities of the work will also enable you to appreciate not only the skills involved but also the time taken, and the costs. Major projects involving electricity and water and structural alterations should always be left to a qualified professional who will be aware of any local building codes or legal requirements often involved with such work. Insurance claims can be affected, or invalidated, if work does not comply with strict regulations cited in the policies. If you live in a historical building or architectural gem, permission may be necessary for any work carried out, and that work will be subjected to scrutiny by the local regulators as well as picky purists.

Don't subject yourself to the risks entailed in the use of high ladders, contact with electricity, gas, or potentially dangerous equipment and materials, hazardous dust, and toxic fumes. Anything that involves lifting or handling heavy weights or large volumes benefits from brawn as well as skill.

Doing it yourself offers great satisfaction and enjoyment as well as the opportunity to save money, but don't be a martyr or feel you are letting down the sisterhood of emancipated women by admitting that you either hate, or just can't do certain jobs and end up calling in a "man." Lack of confidence and skill can lead to a poor or unsuccessful job which not only looks awful but can be costly to put right. It's far easier to admire someone for their level-headedness and level shelves than to sympathize with a do-it-all know-it-all with singed eyebrows, cuts and bruises from their latest do-it-yourself disaster.

jobs best left to the professionals

Even if you have reluctantly "called in the experts" the chances are that it won't be long before you begin to feel very relieved that you hadn't decided to do it yourself. If you are still not convinced, try lifting a bag of cement or wheeling a barrow full of rubble up a steeply sloping plank!

structural changes

Anything involving the structure of your home should always be referred to an expert as it can be unclear what is holding what up, and in extreme cases the removal of an apparently useless post can be disastrous.

It may even be necessary to obtain permission for relatively small jobs such as opening up a wall between two rooms, so find out about local building codes. The foundations and the load-bearing structures must also be taken into consideration when contemplating new walls and floors, windows and heavy fixtures such as cast iron baths.

An architect or structural engineer will know about these things, can do any calculations relating to weight-bearing needed, will understand local building codes, and can organize relevant inspections.

demolition work

Employ a builder for all demolition and rebuilding work. He can deal with unexpected discoveries such as wiring, pipework, structural faults, and other hidden horrors.

specialist skills

Bricklayers, plasterers, carpenters, electricians, plumbers, painters, and decorators all have the skills and knowledge to work efficiently, safely, speedily, and with a high standard of quality and finish. Good craftsmen are expensive but worth it.

For historical properties you may need to employ specialists in a particular skill, material, method, or process to achieve a professional result that complements your home and also complies with local codes regarding historical buildings.

health hazards

Some building materials such as cement and insulation materials are hazardous or just downright unpleasant to handle. The dust and fumes from sanding, sawing, wood treatments, varnishes, paints, and reconstituted wood are potential health hazards which you may not want to subject yourself to.

Dangerous jobs involving the use of long ladders, scaffolding, or specialist equipment are also best left to professionals.

heavy work

Building materials can be heavy, large, long, or unwieldy. Lumber, sheets of drywall, particleboard, plywood, and rolls of carpet or vinyl won't fit in an average car and, even if you have them delivered, can be difficult to maneuver up stairs.

gas, electricity, and water

Strict regulations cover the installation of gas, electricity, and water supplies. Failure to comply affects any claims on your insurance policy. Using registered professionals will give you some redress should anything go wrong.

Anything to do with electric circuits, rewiring, new outlets, or lighting systems should not be attempted by amateurs. Leave it to the professionals.

getting the best from your handyman

Stories about builders are the staple of dinner party guests, newspaper columnists, and comedians, so it's not surprising that "hiring a contractor" is viewed with fear and trepidation. It is never going to be great having your home turned upside down and taken over by strangers but there are things you can do to minimize the risks of trauma.

first, find your builder

Recommendation is best, preferably by a friend or architect—they are very fussy so unlikely to recommend anyone unreliable—but if you have to make the decision on your own look around your neighborhood for current building works, note the state of the site (and the builders themselves), and if you are impressed, ask them to visit and quote for your work. Ask if you can look at a recent job and if possible speak to the previous clients.

the quote

Your new-found knowledge of home improvement should help you understand, and appreciate, the complexities of a job. Before the builder arrives make a list of exactly what needs to be done, together with a plan or drawing if relevant. Inspect the site of the work with the builder so that you are both aware of all aspects involved in the job and any problems that may arise. Quotes can be based on an hourly rate plus materials or a single figure for the whole job (often there isn't a choice as builders usually work on one or the other). Make sure that the quote includes the cost of removing all building refuse and, if possible, an estimated cost of materials. Specify exact colors, materials, and finishes to be used. Always get quotes in writing, preferably on headed stationery and double-check to make sure everything is included.

Setting a completion date involves a mix of realism, fantasy, and wishful thinking. Unforeseen problems from the late delivery of a tub to the discovery of Roman remains can slow down progress, so be prepared to be patient. If you accept the unwritten rule that any building work ends up costing twice as much and takes three times longer than the original estimates, you will not feel too aggrieved when things don't go according to plan.

terms of engagement

In order to avoid upsets and misunderstandings discuss methods of payment, working times, access, storage of equipment, materials and refuse, plus any rules you wish to impose. Establish how payment will be made. Some builders pay their employees weekly and you may be asked for an advance of money for materials—but don't pay the last installment until the work is completed to your satisfaction.

Make sure they can store materials and equipment in a secured area and check that no refuse or materials are obstructing roads or access for other occupants. If you live in an apartment, the other tenants may not appreciate banging at 8 o'clock in the morning, so ask them to start with quiet jobs.

preparation

Clear everything possible from the area where work is to take place. Remove breakables and take down drapes and shades. Make sure your builder provides protection for surfaces. Floors are especially vulnerable. Plastic or canvas drop cloths are not always enough,

sometimes floors may need to be covered by plywood sheets.

safety

Good builders will employ good safety practices. Many choose not to wear masks or hard hats and secure their ladders, but while you may think this is their problem not yours, be warned! The local building codes can be complex, so in order to avoid worries over liability for property and people, make it your business to find out about them.

work in progress

If you are out during the day, inspect the day's work carefully each evening and note any poor workmanship, deviations from the specified job, or materials. If you are out, call at least once a day (but don't overdo it) and ask for a progress report. Give them your contact number at work so they can get in touch regarding any problems, choice of materials, etc. If you are at home, don't peer over their shoulder while they work. Keep an eagle eye on them in more subtle ways by taking them refreshments and engaging in banter on the pleasures of

good craftsmanship and the mysteries of why things never look perfectly straight to the untrained eye!

It is rare that a job is limited to the original brief. Extras arise through unforeseen problems or additional, "while you're here can you just do..." works. Ask for a daily update on extra work undertaken including estimated additional cost in time, labor, and materials.

good relations

You are employing builders because they can do things that you can't, so treat them with respect. It is surprising how many apparently mild-mannered people turn into demanding, snooty, unreasonable monsters when dealing with workmen. Builders are far more likely to do a decent job for a decent person who is pleasant and appreciative, so even if you have a legitimate grievance choose civilized negotiation rather than hysterical rant.

The common complaint about builders is that they take a long time to do things and take too many breaks—but how long do you wait before your first cup of coffee at the office? Building

work is physically demanding, so it is unrealistic to expect them to keep going at top speed for eight hours a day and there will be times when they are waiting for things to dry, someone else to finish their job or deliveries to arrive.

They may leave early if they have come to the end of one job and there is not enough time to start the next, and although this makes progress seem frustratingly slow, consider how much of your working day you spend actually working between coffee and lunch breaks, personal phone calls, chatting, gossiping, or just daydreaming!

However, don't be too soft and don't put up with poor workmanship. Show that you expect some respect, too, and that you know about building work despite being female. Most builders are men but don't play the helpless female, and don't flirt; this could lead to misunderstandings. Instead, show you mean business by being firm but fair and conducting yourself in a businesslike, but good-humored, manner.

in your dreams

It's easy to be bitten by the do it yourself bug. Relaxing in your much-improved interior, sipping champagne to celebrate another job well done, all memories of dust and mess forgotten, you are enjoying the luxury of having shelves for your books and a hook on the back of the door for your bathrobe, then, popping into the kitchen for a few nibbles, your newly critical eyes are drawn to the ill-fitting cabinet door, the slightly chipped countertop, the inadequate storage, the dated design.... And before you know it, you have settled back on the couch with the nibbles, another glass of bubbly, and a pile of interiors magazines, brochures, and catalogs, and are busily planning a new kitchen which you will, of course, be installing all by yourself.

Of course we are allowed to dream, and sometimes, with patience, determination, energy, and a healthy dose of down-to-earth, practical, common-sense, we can turn those dreams into reality. In home improvement terms a little knowledge is a useful, rather than a dangerous, thing and if you are a dab hand at putting together self-assembly furniture and a whizz at drilling holes and

putting up support boards, th
you have all the skills necess
putting in a new kitchen.

In practice, the classic ni
experiences of wobbly walls,
floors, and falling ceilings car
easily become the all-too-rea
living horror story. However, u
newly aquired knowledge of
matters you should be able t
predict the possible pitfalls o
on such a project. Of course
champagne has worn off you
see the sense of "getting sor
And when you trip over the s
again on your way to bed, it
dreaming about a nice shed
in the garden, with a proper
workbench, rows of tools,
and an impressive collection
of equipment from power
drills to saws and sanders.

Just think, you could
spend many happy hours
in your fully equipped
workroom making pipe-
racks and book-ends while
the builder gets on with
fitting your new kitchen!

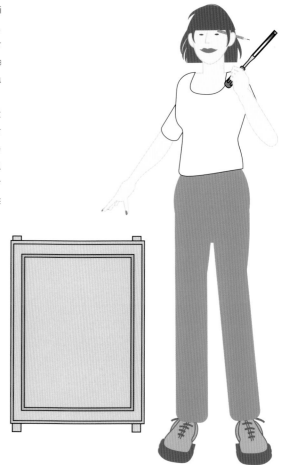

Useful Addresses

Home Improvement Stores

Do It Best
www.doitbest.com
stores throughout the US

The Home Depot
www.homedepot.com
stores throughout the US

Lowe's
www.lowes.com
stores throughout the US

Architectural Salvage and Reclamation

Salvo! USA
www.salvoweb.com
directory of suppliers of architectural salvage

Architectural Salvage Inc.
3 Mill Street, Exeter, NH 03833
tel (603) 773 5635
www.oldhousesalvage.com
architectural salvage bought and sold

The Old House Web
216 Brunswick Avenue, Gardiner, ME 04345
tel (207) 582 2162
www.theoldhouseweb.com
directory of suppliers of architectural salvage

Bathrooms

Eurobath & Tile
Stonemill Design Center, 2915 Redhill Avenue, Suite F102, Costa Mesa, CA 92626
tel (714) 545 2284
www.eurobathtile.com
bathroom and kitchen fixtures

Fireworks Tiles
9 Wilson Street, Amissville, VA 20106
tel (540) 937 8944
www.fireworkstiles.com
handpainted ceramic tiles

Winstar
1252 Hibiscus Lane, Apopka, FL 32703
tel (407) 869 9469
www.winstar.org
bathroom and kitchen products

Fabrics

Brunschwig & Fils
www.brunschwig.com
fabrics and accessories; showrooms throughout the US

Designers Guild
(c/o Osborne & Little Inc.)
www.designersguild.com
contemporary fabrics, wallpaper, furniture, and accessories

F. Schumacher & Co.
79 Madison Avenue, New York, NY 10016
tel (212) 415 3900
www.fschumacher.com
decorative fabrics and wallpaper

Lee Jofa Inc.
201 Central Avenue South, Bethpage, New York, NY 11714
tel (800) 453 3563
www.leejofa.com
decorative fabrics and wallpaper

Osborne & Little Inc.
979 Third Avenue, Suite 520, New York, NY 10022
tel (212) 751 3333
www.osborneandlittle.com
decorative fabrics; stockists throughout the US

Zoffany
979 Third Avenue, Suite 1403, New York, NY 10022
tel (212) 593 9787
www.zoffany.com
decorative fabrics and wallpaper; showrooms throughout the US

Floors

ABC Carpet & Home
881 Broadway, New York, NY10003
tel (212) 473 3000
or
777 South Congress, Delray Beach, FL 33445
tel (561) 279 7777
www.abchome.com
natural floorings, including coir, sisal, seagrass, jute, and wool

Bedrosians
4285 N. Golden State Blvd, Fresno, CA 93722-6316
tel (559) 275 5000
www.bedrosians.com
ceramic tile and natural stone

Craftsman Lumber Co. Inc.
435 Main Street, PO Box 222, Groton, MA 01450
tel (978) 448 5621
www.craftsmanlumber.com
pine and oak flooring

Hosking Hardwood Flooring
PO Box 163, Walpole, MA 02081
tel (508) 668 8315
www.hoskinghardwood.com

James E. Harvey Millwork Inc.
PO Box 249, 22665 River Ridge Road, Bozman, MD 21612-0249
tel (410) 822 7689
www.harveymillwork.com
custom flooring and paneling

Pergo, Inc.
Attention: Consumer Affairs, 3128 Highwoods Blvd., Suite 100, Raleigh, NC 27604
tel (800) 337 3746
www.pergo.com
laminate flooring

Simpson Stone Tile
423 W. Columbia Street, Orlando, FL 32825
tel (407) 481 1066
reproductions with the natural looks of slate, terra cotta, etc.

Kitchens

Aga Ranges LLC
110 Woodcrest Road, Cherry Hill, NJ 08003
tel (800) 633 9200
www.aga-ranges.com
showrooms throughout the US

Alno
A.N.U., One Design Center Place, Suite 643, Boston, MA 02210
tel (617) 482 2566
www.alno.com
German manufacturer with showrooms throughout the US

Balthaup Kitchens
www.balthaup.com
showrooms throughout the US

Chalon
c/o Oliver Walker & Company, 1855 Griffin Road, Suite A423, Dania, FL 33004
tel (954) 929 0031
www.chalon.com
showrooms throughout the US

Gaggenau
tel (800) 294 0644
www.gaggenau.com
built-in appliances

IKEA
www.ikea-usa.com
*stockists throughout the US;
some products available online*

Plain and Simple Kitchens
Kitchen Living LLC,
One Design Center Place,
Suite 620, Boston, MA 02210
tel (617) 439 8800
www.plainandsimplekitchens.com

Restoration Hardware
711 Boylston Street, Boston,
MA 02116
tel (617) 578 0088
www.restorationhardware.com
*functional and decorative hardware, plus home furnishings –
retail and online shopping*

SieMatic
www.siematic.com
showrooms throughout the US

Watts and Wright
tel +44 (8) 700 110 130
www.wattsandwright.com
bespoke cabinetmakers

Williams-Sonoma
Stanford Shopping Center
180 El Camino Real
Palo Alto, CA 94304
tel (650) 321 3486
www.williams-sonoma.com
*kitchen equipment and home
furnishings; available online
and by mail order*

Lighting and Furniture

The Bon Marché
1601 Third Avenue, Seattle,
WA 98181
tel (206) 506 6000
www.thebonmarche.com
*furniture, lighting, fabrics, and
accessories*

The Craftsman Homes
Connection
PMB 343, 2525 E. 29th
Street, Suite 10B, Spokane,
WA 99223
tel (509) 535 5098
www.crafthome.com

The Conran Shop
Bridgemarket, 407 East 59th
Street, New York, NY 10022
tel (212) 755 9079
www.conran.com
modern furniture, lighting, fabrics and accessories

Ethan Allen
PO Box 1966, Danbury, CT
0681-1966
tel (203) 743 8000
www.ethanallen.com

Isgro & Company
3248 Sacramento Avenue,
San Francisco, CA 94115
tel (415) 931 5858
*antique lighting, restoration,
repair, and design*

Ligne Roset
250 Park Avenue, New York,
NY 10003
tel (212) 375 1036
www.ligne-roset.com
www.lignerosetny.com
*French furniture and design,
outlets throughout the US*

Macy's West
170 O'Farrell Street, San
Francisco, CA 94102
tel (415) 397 3333
www.macys.com
*furniture, lighting, fabrics, and
accessories*

Pier 1 Imports
tel (800) 447 4371
outlets throughout the US

The Pottery Barn
tel (888) 779 5176
www.potterybarn.com

The Renovator's Supply
Renovator's Old Mill,
Millers Falls, MA 01349
tel (800) 659 2211
www.renovatorssupply.com
mail order and online

W.D. Bosworth Woodworking
& Sculpture
59 Luther Warren Drive,
St Helena Island, SC 29920
tel (843) 838 9490
www.qualitywoodworking.com
quality custom made furniture

Rejuvenation Lamp & Fixture Co.
2550 NW Nicolai Street,
Portland, Or 97210
tel (888) 343 8548
www.rejuvenation.com
period lighting

Paints

Sanderson & Sons Ltd
Suite 409, 979 Third Avenue,
New York, NY 10022
tel (212) 319 7220
www.sanderson-uk.com
*traditional English paints and
wallpapers, including William
Morris prints*

Benjamin Moore & Co.
51 Chestnut Ridge Road,
Montvale, NJ 07645
tel (800) 344 0400
www.benjaminmoore.com
*to use their online colour
selector*

The Old Fashioned Milk Paint
Co. Inc
436 Main Street, Groton, MA
01450

tel (978) 448 6336
www.milkpaint.com
*building or restoring Colonial or
Shaker furniture*

Farrow and Ball
www.farrow-ball.com
*traditional paints and wallpapers;
buy direct from the UK or US
stockists*

Paint and Paper Library
Fonthill Ltd, 979 Third Avenue,
New York, NY 10022
tel (212) 755 6700
www.paintlibrary.com
*paints and wallpapers by
Neisha Crosland, Emily
Todhunter, David Oliver, and
Nina Campbell (paint only)*

Planning

American Architectural Directory
www.architects-in-america.com
*listings for architects and
interior designers*

www.theinteriordesigner.com
*directory of suppliers and
interior design professionals*

Windows

Anna French
Classic Revivials Inc, One
Design Center Place, Suite
534, Boston, MA 02210
tel (617) 574 9030
www.anna-french.demon.co.uk

Rosso Objekte
c/o Design Syntax, 3525 Old
Conejo Road, Suite 107,
Newbury Park, CA
tel (805) 498 4747
www.rosso-objekte.com
modern curtain fixing systems

Index

Author's Acknowledgments

Producing a book is very much a team effort so many thanks to the Quadrille team: to Jane O'Shea for asking me to do it; to Mary Evans for making me do things I thought I couldn't (and keeping everyone on their toes with her legendary attention to detail); to Lisa Pendreigh, the perfect editor who organized the text with a winning combination of good sense and humor; to Coralie, Jim, and Katy, the book designers who used creativity and technological wizardry to make it all happen; and to Helen Lewis for art-directing great photography. And a special mention to Ernie and Michael who managed to make "having the builders in" an enjoyable experience and also provided good advice and useful hints for the book.

Publisher's Acknowledgments

The publisher has made every effort to trace the copyright holders, architects, and designers featured in this book. We apologize in advance for any unintentional omission and would be pleased to insert the appropriate acknowledgment in any subsequent edition.

8–20 Graham Atkins Hughes; 25 © Elle Decoration/Neil Mersh/Amanda Smith; 34–39 Graham Atkins Hughes; 44 Sanoma Syndication/Dennis Brandsma; 49 Vega MG/Giulio Oriani/architect Elisabetta Pincherle/Studio 98; 50 IPC Syndication/© Living Etc./David Loftus; 56–62 Graham Atkins Hughes; 68 above The Interior Archive/Tim Beddow/designer Melissa Stephenson; 68 below Ray Main/Mainstream; 69 above Sanoma Syndication/Hotze Eisma; 69 below Taverne Agency/Hans Zeegers/production Olga Serrarens/www.greetedewilde.com; 70 Graham Atkins Hughes; 76 above Hotze Eisma; 76 below IPC Syndication/Janine Hosegood; 77 above David Hiscock; 77 below IPC Syndication/Janine Hosegood; 79 Graham Atkins Hughes; 82 Dominic Blackmore/designer Angela A'Court; 86 Graham Atkins Hughes; 94 © Résidences Décoration/Alain Sauvan; 95 Narratives/Jan Baldwin/bags by Somogyvari (helen@somogyvari.com); 97 The Interior Archive/Edina van der Wyck/designer Atlanta Bartlett; 100 Graham Atkins Hughes; 103 Red Cover/Winfried Heinze; 104–105 IPC Syndication/© Homes & Gardens/Geoffrey Young; 106 above Richard Foster; 106 below International Interiors/Paul Ryan/designers Kastrup & Sjunnesson; 107 above Hotze Eisma; 107 below International Interiors/Paul Ryan/designer Eugenie Voorhees; 108–135 Graham Atkins Hughes.